...blished
...brands,
...travel.

...ars our
...secrets
...world,
sharing with travellers a wealth of
experience and a passion for travel.

**Rely on Thomas Cook as your
travelling companion on your next trip
and benefit from our unique heritage.**

Thomas Cook **pocket** guides

STOCKHOLM

Your travelling companion since 1873

Thomas
Cook

Written by Barbara Radcliffe Rogers & Stillman Rogers
Updated by Maria Lundqvist

Published by Thomas Cook Publishing
A division of Thomas Cook Tour Operations Limited
Company registration No: 3772199 England
The Thomas Cook Business Park, 9 Coningsby Road
Peterborough PE3 8SB, United Kingdom
Email: books@thomascook.com, Tel: +44 (0)1733 416477
www.thomascookpublishing.com

Produced by The Content Works Ltd
Aston Court, Kingsmead Business Park, Frederick Place
High Wycombe, Bucks HP11 1LA
www.thecontentworks.com

Series design based on an original concept by Studio 183 Limited

ISBN: 978-1-84848-288-3

First edition © 2006 Thomas Cook Publishing
This third edition © 2010 Thomas Cook Publishing
Text © Thomas Cook Publishing
Maps © Thomas Cook Publishing/PCGraphics (UK) Limited
Transport map © Communicarta Limited

Series Editor: Kelly Anne Pipes
Production/DTP: Steven Collins

Printed and bound in Spain by GraphyCems

Cover photography (The Old City) © Deco/Alamy

CONTENTS

SYMBOLS KEY

The following symbols are used throughout this book:

ⓐ address ⓣ telephone ⓦ website address ⓛ opening times
Ⓝ public transport connections ❶ important

The following symbols are used on the maps:

𝒊 information office		▢	points of interest
✈ airport		O	city
✚ hospital		O	large town
🛡 police station		○	small town
▤ bus station		=	motorway
▤ railway station		—	main road
Ⓜ metro		—	minor road
✝ cathedral		—	railway
❶ numbers denote featured cafés & restaurants			

Hotels and restaurants are graded by approximate price as follows:
£ budget price ££ mid-range price £££ expensive

▶ *Aerial view with Stockholm's spires and shimmering waters*

INTRODUCING
Stockholm

Introduction

Stockholm wraps its arms around its small harbours, embracing the fleet of white ferries that slips continually in and out of their grasp. The sea and the city are inseparable. Nearly every cityscape is either reflected in or framed by water, and neighbourhoods are defined by the 14 islands on which they are built.

Getting from one place to another usually means crossing a bridge, but will also likely involve crossing a park. The former vegetable garden of the Royal Palace, in the heart of the shopping district, is a park, and others appear at every turn. Only minutes from the centre, the island of Djurgården is a vast park, studded here and there with museums and attractions, but essentially green. Locals are fond of pointing out that Stockholm is one third water, one third green belt and one third city.

The other thing that visitors notice is that Stockholm is an intensely Swedish city, more representative of the country as a whole than most capitals are, and at every turn is another example of the Swedish design that people here value so dearly.

This is a very visual city, its buildings well kept, its streets clean, its parks and gardens manicured, its people well dressed and its squares adorned with public art. It is also a very walkable city, easy to explore on foot, with its sights close together, its neighbourhoods well defined and plenty of cafés and park benches to break the journey. Because the city is so attractive, you will want to explore it on foot, enjoying the sudden surprises as a street opens onto the water, or the turn of a corner brings you into a square surrounded by elegant buildings and adorned with sculpture.

It would be a shame, however, to treat Stockholm as just another pretty face. There's far more to it than that, so be sure to allow time to meet the locals and to join in local activities. Jog along the water's edge in the morning, take a ferry to a small island, stop for coffee in cafés, sit on the grass for a free concert or step up to the bar in a neighbourhood pub. You'll soon find yourself part of the exciting milieu that is Stockholm.

◆ *Enjoy the city's café culture and traditional architecture in Gamla Stan*

When to go

SEASONS & CLIMATE

Scandinavian summers are short, but intense, with long daylight hours lasting well into the night. You have a better chance of having a holiday filled with sunlit days if you travel in June and July. From the Midsummer celebrations in June through late July is when most Swedes take holidays, so expect the archipelago to be crowded.

The season when attractions keep the longest hours, and when smaller ones are open daily, begins in early June and ends in mid-August. Many smaller attractions will add a few weeks of weekends-only opening in spring and autumn.

Spring and autumn are pleasant, with uncertain weather. Winter is long, lasting from November through to March. Daylight hours are short then, but weather often tends to be clear and crisp, with bright white snow glimmering in the dark city. While many archipelago lodgings and restaurants close in the winter, a few are open. But be sure to book ahead, since boats are fewer and many places open only when they have guests arriving. Stockholm rocks on all winter, with the action moving inside to cosier surroundings.

ANNUAL EVENTS

Most offices, banks and shops – even restaurants – close for public holidays. Banks may also close the day before a holiday. A full calendar of month-by-month events is listed at Ⓦ www.stockholmtown.com and Ⓦ www.sweden.se

January

New Year's Concert The Storkyrkan Chamber Orchestra and Chorus perform Beethoven's Ninth Symphony at the Cathedral of Stockholm. ⓐ Trångsund 1 ⓣ 08 723 3016; tickets: 077 170 7070 Ⓦ www.stockholmsdomkyrkoforsamling.se

February
Stockholm Furniture Fair The world's largest meeting place for Nordic design. Held annually at the Stockholm International Fairs in Älvsjö.
❶ 08 749 4100 ⓦ http://furniture.stofair.se

April
Easter Easter Saturday is the main day for celebrating with dinner parties and the exchanging of sweet-filled Easter eggs, but all homes and shops are decorated with feather-clad branches of birch, weeks before this major Swedish holiday.

Walpurgis Night (30 April) A public holiday celebrated throughout Sweden with bonfires and choral singing. Major festivities in Stockholm are on the terrace at Riddarholmen, or in Skansen Park (admission charged). See ⓦ www.stockholmtown.com for other locations.

May
May Day Public holiday observed by the rallies and gatherings of the Social Democratic Party, left-leaning political parties and action groups.

Opera and ballet Opening of the summer season of opera and ballet, which runs through June. Kungliga Operan (Royal Swedish Opera) Box Office ❶ 08 791 4400 ⓦ www.operan.se

June
A Taste of Stockholm Restaurants set up booths in Kungsträdgården for an entire week, selling samples of their specialities; a great way to try dishes from fine restaurants without having to buy a whole meal.
ⓦ www.smakapastockholm.se

Stockholm Marathon International runners have been invading the streets of Stockholm for over 30 years now. Prepare for difficult access throughout town. ⓦ www.stockholmmarathon.se

Parkteatern Free performances until August that range from circus to dance and music, held in public parks. ❶ 08 506 20200
ⓦ www.stadsteatern.stockholm.se

National Day (6 June) A public holiday, introduced in 2005, celebrated with an evening programme at Skansen Park, with bands, ceremony and entertainment attended by the Swedish Royal Family.
Midsummer's Eve, Midsummer's Day Public holidays, celebrated throughout the country with cookouts, picnics and family gatherings (see page 12).

July
Stockholm Jazz Festival World-rated artists perform all kinds of jazz on Skeppsholmen. ❶ 077 170 7070 ❼ www.stockholmjazz.com

August
Stockholm Pride Scandinavia's largest gay festival.
❼ www.stockholmpride.org
Midnattsloppet Thousands of runners compete in a late-night race through Södermalm, a grand excuse for everyone else to party all night. ❶ 08 649 7171 ❼ www.midnattsloppet.com
Cultural Festival of Stockholm A five-day festival with over 300 attractions around the city, from music and theatre to markets and exhibitions. ❶ 08 508 31900 ❼ www.kulturfestivalen.stockholm.se

September
Musik på Slottet Evening concerts of classical, folk and jazz music continue through September inside the Royal Palace. ❶ 077 170 7070 ❼ www.royalfestivals.se

October
Stockholm Open Annual ATP tournament with international tennis stars. ❼ www.stockholmopen.se

November
Stockholm International Film Festival Hundreds of films from all

over the world, showcased at cinemas across town. Also seminars and visiting international stars. Ⓦ www.filmfestivalen.se

December
Christmas Markets Kungsträdgården, Skansen Park, Rosendal Palace and Stortorget all host holiday craft markets.
Nobel Day On 10 December, the King of Sweden awards the Nobel Prize and the Nobel Banquet is held. Descend on City Hall to catch a glimpse of the festivities and the arriving luminaries. Ⓦ http://nobelprize.org
Lucia (13 Dec) A once heathen ritual is now a joyous celebration of light in the darkest month of the year.
Nyårsafton (New Year's Eve Celebration) The old year is rung out with live music and fireworks at Skansen Outdoor Museum.
Ⓘ 08 442 8000 (info 24 hours) Ⓦ www.skansen.se

PUBLIC HOLIDAYS

New Year's Day 1 Jan	17 May 2012, 9 May 2013
Epiphany 6 Jan	**Whit Sunday** 12 June 2011,
Maundy Thursday 21 Apr 2011,	27 May 2012, 19 May 2013
5 Apr 2012, 28 Mar 2013	**National Day** 6 June
Good Friday 22 Apr 2011,	**Midsummer's Eve & Day** 25 &
6 Apr 2012, 29 Mar 2013	26 June 2010, 24 & 25 June
Easter Sunday 24 Apr 2011,	2011, 22 & 23 June 2012
8 Apr 2012, 31 Mar 2013	**All Saints Day** 6 Nov 2010,
Easter Monday 25 Apr 2011,	5 Nov 2011, 3 Nov 2012
9 Apr 2012, 1 Apr 2013	**Christmas Eve** 24 Dec
Walpurgis Night 30 Apr	**Christmas Day** 25 Dec
May Day 1 May	**Boxing Day** 26 Dec
Ascension Day 2 June 2011,	**New Year's Eve** 31 Dec

Midsommar

At the summer solstice, when the days are longest and nights shortest, Sweden celebrates Midsummer's Eve. The holiday is no longer precisely on the solstice, but has been set at the third Friday and Saturday of June, so families can enjoy the weekend together. It's an occasion to go to a country house or a cottage on the archipelago, or to simply take a picnic to the countryside or a park.

A maypole – *majstång* in Swedish – is at the centre of the most traditional celebrations, a tall pole decorated with garlands of leaves and flowers. The decorated pole is raised and everyone sings or dances beneath it. Flower crowns are another tradition, woven of fresh flowers. Both of these customs arise in ancient pagan festivals celebrating the summer and hoping for abundant harvests, but today Midsummer's Eve is a good excuse for a day in the country and a good party.

The traditional foods are new potatoes with dill and pickled herring or smoked fish in infinite variety, accompanied by beer and schnapps, topped off by the season's first strawberries for dessert.

Although many Swedes celebrate at private gatherings of family and friends, there are plenty of public activities where visitors can join in. Any farm museum will have a celebration with a maypole and in Stockholm, Skansen Park celebrates for three days. Visitors help make the flower garlands that decorate the maypole, and can join in the dancing after it is raised. It's particularly colourful there because many people are in traditional costume. It's also a good chance to hear folk songs and see traditional dances.

The Skansen Folk Dance Team performs and fiddlers play traditional tunes for the ring dances around the maypole and for the singing that follows. Folk dance displays continue into the evening and everyone dances on Skansen Park's outdoor dance floors.

More intimate parties go on at some country inns, especially at Grinda Wärdshus, the island country house on Grinda (see page 135), in the archipelago. You can gather wildflowers there and someone will be on hand to show you how to weave a flower crown to wear for the festivities. It's a popular place, so reserve early for that weekend (ⓦ www.grindawardshus.se).

⬤ *Wildflowers are woven into a crowning glory at Midsummer festivities*

History

While the Vikings had a thriving city on the nearby island of Birka at the turn of the second millennium, Stockholm's history begins in 1252 when Birger Jarl began building Tre Kronor fortress. The city continued to grow, with a setback from the plague in the mid-14th century, until Sweden's entry into the Kalmar Union, which united all four Scandinavian states. Rebellion followed rebellion as the Swedes fought to be free of this Danish domination, including the infamous Stockholm Bloodbath of 1520, when the Danish king beheaded more than 80 leaders of this opposition.

Finally, three years later, Gustav Vasa defeated the Danes and became King of the newly freed Sweden. But the Danes didn't give up so easily, and the wars continued on and off for decades. Meanwhile, Protestantism took hold in Sweden, and the state confiscated the monasteries and church property. Throughout the 1600s, Stockholm expanded, spilling over onto more islands, but the Great Northern War, against an alliance of most of its neighbours, resulted in the loss of much of Sweden's territory. While this was going on, Parliament reduced the power of the king, creating a parliamentary state. By the end of the 1700s, King Gustav III had restored the crown's power, which got him shot at a masquerade ball, and Parliament regained control.

The middle of the 19th century was a difficult time for Sweden, with economic depression prompting waves of emigration to the USA and movement of rural Swedes into Stockholm. Sweden managed to retain neutrality as World War I raged through the rest of Europe, while political unrest at home resulted in universal voting rights. In World War II, Sweden again remained officially neutral, though it couldn't stop Nazi forces crossing the country on their way to defeat and subdue Norway.

In the 1950s city officials, as part of their plan to make Stockholm a modern city, began the T-bana underground transit system and the systematic demolition of historic neighbourhoods, which were replaced with severe concrete buildings. Now deemed a mistake, this wholesale destruction changed the face of Stockholm dramatically. Massive protests finally succeeded in blocking further destruction in 1975, sparing those parts that had remained undamaged.

Other social and political changes were also afoot. The monarchy was finally stripped of all political power in 1974, and immigration to Sweden that had begun in the 1960s began to create social problems unknown in hitherto homogeneous Sweden. In 1995 Sweden joined the EU, following an economic depression and devaluation of the krona.

Today, Sweden continues to cope with the heavy tax burdens of its welfare state, but takes pride in a healthy population and progressive policies regarding social, environmental and cultural issues. A centre-right government ousted the long-standing Social Democrats from power in 2006, emphasising free markets and privatization without compromising on the welfare system. In light of the global economic meltdown of 2008–9, however, it remains to be seen how long their policies, and popularity, will last.

Lifestyle

Stockholm is well known as one of Europe's most 'live and let live' cities, with an open gay and lesbian scene and an anything-goes nightlife marred only by archaic laws concerning dancing in bars.

Although all this might make the city sound wide open, it is really quite orderly. It is also one of Europe's safest cities, largely because of the Swedish respect for moderation and 'the way things should be' and their high-mindedness about the public good. Not only does Stockholm have a low crime rate (even in the underground transit system), but its air is clean and its waters unpolluted.

If Stockholm is refreshingly free of the seedy underbelly of so many cities, its opposite is also missing. Nothing here seems over the top or outrageous, perhaps because of the ingrained Swedish sense of *lagom*. The word translates roughly to 'only enough' – and it underlies the national appreciation of understatement, restraining the temptation to be ostentatious in any way.

So while Stockholm residents play hard, they are basically well behaved and respectful of each other, of visitors and of differences.

Perhaps more even than the shared sense of *lagom*, the glue that holds Stockholm society together is coffee. The coffee break is a national institution, and cafés are alive and well – everywhere you look. People even seem to stop for a cup on their way to meet a friend for coffee.

Gay and lesbian travellers have their own section on the tourist board's website: go to ⓦ www.visitsweden.com/stockholm and click on 'Gay Stockholm' to find a host of useful information and links. The city's Gay Pride celebration in early August is a boisterous, colourful event, the largest of its kind in Scandinavia. The free newspaper *QX* is a good source of events listings for gay-friendly bars and clubs, as is their website ⓦ www.qx.se.

🔺 *Enjoy an alfresco lunch in one of the city's many seaside cafés*

Culture

Stockholm's cultural life is rich and varied, with something for all tastes, from grand opera to cutting-edge contemporary art. And even the most high-brow event is not reserved for the rich and privileged.

The season for the Kungliga Operan (Royal Opera House, see page 81) and for the philharmonic and symphony orchestras at Stockholms Konserthus (Stockholm Concert Hall, see page 81) is September to May. In the summer, seek outdoor venues for concerts and music festivals. The Royal Opera House is also the stage used for the Royal Ballet, which usually performs traditional ballet classics. For more edgy and contemporary operas and avant-garde productions, look to the Folkoperan (see page 118). Theatre performances, unfortunately, are almost all in Swedish.

For up-to-date listings of performance schedules, see the free magazine *What's on Stockholm*, available at hotels and tourist offices, or look at the events listings by month on the city's tourism website ⓦ www.stockholmtown.com

Tickets are available either online through websites of individual venues or at Kulturhuset (see page 66).

Along with performing arts and music, Stockholm is filled with visual arts, from outstanding public sculpture to its art museums and galleries.

Design is an obsession with Swedes, with exhibitions, shows, commissioned works, new buildings and other initiatives continually spotlighting contemporary designers and artists. A host of design-related initiatives in recent years have helped to heighten awareness of the unique role Sweden has played, and will surely continue to play, in the world of design.

◑ Carl Milles' impressive Orpheus welcomes you to Stockholms Konserthus

ABBA

The whole world knows Abba, the pop group that burst onto the scene in the 1970s by winning the Eurovision Song Contest with *Waterloo*. At the height of their stride in the late 1970s they were Sweden's biggest export, exceeding even Volvo. Although they disbanded in 1983, their popularity continues, their 350 million record sales and continued placement on the UK charts 20 years later making them second only to the Beatles in all-time popularity. They remain the epitome of 1970s style, the quintessence of glam pop. In 2005 the group appeared together in public for the first time since 1986 for the Swedish première of Mamma Mia!, their hit musical that was subsequently turned into a major motion picture starring Meryl Streep and Swedish actor Stellan Skarsgård.

Art galleries abound in Östermalm and Södermalm, while the latest gathering point for emerging artists is in Hornstull, at Södermalm's western edge, and on Huddiksvallsgatan. Galleries traditionally close in summer, reopening in mid-August. For news on galleries, openings and shows, search the calendar on Ⓦ www.stockholmtown.com or read the art listings in *What's On Stockholm*, downloadable from the same website.

▶ *The Royal Palace by night*

MAKING THE MOST OF
Stockholm

Shopping

Swedish design is known for innovation and flair, and the graceful beauty of Swedish glassware has made names like Orrefors and Kosta Boda familiar worldwide. Along with design items (for the newest from young unknowns, browse DesignTorget), traditional Nordic jumpers are less expensive here than at home. Knitters excel at well-designed caps and hats, often in striking colours, and children's styles that are clever and practical. Prices on outdoor equipment are good in this land where everyone looks as though they compete in triathlons every Sunday morning.

Hand-forged knives, works of art with carved wood or bone handles (pack them in check-through baggage), are another good, though pricey bet. Look for Kalikå in Gamla Stan and elsewhere for puppets and marionettes, costumes and beautifully made cookware and shop tools scaled for small hands. Children (and many adults) are fascinated by Norsemen, so consider Viking books, replicas and models.

Stockholm's main shopping streets spread from Hötorget to Gamla Stan, centring on Drottninggatan, along Kungsgatan to Stureplan and the length of Birger Jarlsgatan. Gamla Stan attracts tourists with antique stores and craft galleries, while Södermalm draws Stockholm's young and hip to streets around Götgatan and the area south of Folkungagatan, also known as SoFo.

NK is the department store with all the big designers; Åhléns City the less pricey but equally good equivalent. PUB is noted for its designer fashion floor named Awesome Rags! Hötorget is a square filled with colourful flower stalls, where Stockholmers look for bargain bouquets just before dinnertime. Shop hours are fairly standard, 10.00–18.00 or 19.00 Monday to Friday and 10.00–16.00 on Saturdays.

USEFUL SHOPPING PHRASES

What time do they open/close?
När öppnar/stänger ni?
Naehr uhp-nahr/stainger nih?

How much is it?
Hur mycket kostar det?
Huhr muhcket kostar deh?

I'd like to buy ...
Jag skulle vilja ha ...
Yahg skulleh vilyah hah ...

Most stores in the central shopping district, especially chain stores such as H&M and Zara, and department stores like NK, are also open on Sundays from around 11.00–17.00, with smaller boutiques only open for a couple of hours (12.00–15.00) if at all.

Sweden's whopping 25 per cent VAT supports its famously broad social programmes, and if you are from an EU country, be prepared to contribute to it yourself. If not, ask for a VAT refund form whenever the total exceeds SEK200 at any shop. When you leave Sweden, take the items and invoices to the airport customs desk for validation. On arrival home, send these invoices to each store for your tax refund. Each cheque will come in Swedish currency and may well cost you more than its value to cash or deposit. Much easier is Global Refund Service. Ask for a refund cheque at any shop displaying a 'Tax Free' logo. At the airport, have these stamped at the Global Refund Desk and collect your refund in cash.

Eating & drinking

Swedish cooking is much more than meatballs and *gravad lax*. Hot young chefs have donned their toques, fusing highly flavourful local ingredients with cooking styles pulled from all over the world. The short growing season and long summer daylight hours intensify the flavours of berries and vegetables, elevating the humble potato to new heights and turning strawberries into juicy sweets.

Swedish chefs shine brightest with garden-fresh vegetables and the readily available coldwater fish and shellfish from surrounding seas. Add autumn woodland mushrooms, wild lingonberries and cloudberries from the northern bogs, as well as venison – the red meat of choice – and you have the basics of Swedish cuisine.

Innovative Swedish chefs working with these traditional ingredients have led the way in creating a new Nordic cuisine. Stockholm has its share of celebrity chefs, each with a devoted following. Names to note are Erik Lallerstedt at Gondolen, Melker Andersson at Fredsgatan 12, Bocuse d'Or (the world food championships) winner Mathias Dahlgren at Grands Veranda and Pontus Frithiof, chef/owner of Pontus by the Sea and Stureplan newcomer Pontus! Tina Nordström has brought the flavours of

PRICE CATEGORIES

The restaurant price guides used in the book indicate the approximate cost of a main course for one person.

£ up to SEK120   ££ SEK120–220   £££ over SEK220

● *The city's leading restaurants mix traditional dishes with more modern cuisine*

the contemporary Swedish table to world television in her popular series *New Scandinavian Cooking*.

The wave of foreign immigration into Sweden in the 1960s changed Stockholm dining forever. New flavours from the Middle East and Mediterranean crept in and were soon mixed with northern ingredients with brilliant results. More recently chefs began incorporating Asian techniques, especially in preparing the abundant local seafood. In fashion-conscious Stockholm, it's all about what's trendy, so expect anything.

Above all, expect to pay for it. Dining in Stockholm can put a dent in your budget the size of a Volvo. Fortunately, the continental brasserie style has recently taken hold, easing the budget strain a little. The best time to sample the most glamorous places is at lunch, when many offer fixed-price meals. The sign will advertise a *Dagens rätt*, or sometimes *Dagens lunch*.

Main dishes at dinner usually range around SEK150–250 (Asian as low as SEK85), or SEK600–1,000 for set menus. As in most cities, Stockholm's trendier in-spots with designer décor and celebrity chefs are among the priciest, and the neighbourhood places and Asian or Middle Eastern restaurants are the cheapest.

Cafés serve salads and sandwiches and some have all-you-can-eat buffets at lunch. Shopping in markets for picnic foods to take to the park is somewhat difficult, since the food markets in the city centre tend toward gourmet delicacies. But the occasional sandwich shop offers takeout, and you can buy bread and cheese at the Hötorgshallen or Östermalms Saluhall markets or in the supermarkets under major department stores.

In many restaurants, particularly in the tourist areas, menus will offer an English translation alongside the Swedish name. If not, don't be afraid to ask, as most waiters speak at least some English.

À la carte menus offer starters (*förrätter*), main courses (*varmrätter*) and desserts (*desserter*). Many restaurants offer a set menu both at lunch – usually at a special price – and in the evening.

Traditional local dishes include several varieties of pickled herring, blackened herring (*strömming* or *sill*) with potatoes, salmon (*lax*), cured salmon (*gravad lax*), cod (*torsk*), meatballs (*köttbullar*), and

USEFUL DINING PHRASES

I would like a table for ... people, please
Ett bord för ..., tack
Eht boord fuhr ..., tahck

May I see the menu, please?
Kan jag få se menyn, tack?
Kahn yahg foe see mehnewn, tahck?

I am a vegetarian
Jag är vegetarian
Yahg air vehgehtahriahn

Where is the toilet (restroom)?
Var är toaletten?
Vahr air toahlehtehn?

May I have the bill, please?
Jag skulle vilja betala, tack?
Yahg skulleh vilyah behtahlah, tahck?

roasted game meats. Occasionally found on menus, a popular home-style dish known as Jansson's Temptation (*Janssons frestelse*) includes potatoes, onions, butter, anchovies and cream baked together.

Before you even open the wine list, do a mental check on your bank balance. Wines and spirits are notoriously expensive, although not as high as they were before Sweden joined the EU. The most ordinary wine can cost ten times more in a restaurant than its shelf price in the UK or US. In Sweden, you can only buy your own alcohol at state-run stores called *Systembolaget*, which are closed on Sundays. Nor is beer the cheap alternative at upwards of SEK45 a glass. The proper drink with the ubiquitous herring or *gravad lax* is *brännvin* (schnapps), which balances the salty-vinegar flavour of the fish.

◗ *Dusk in Stockholm and bars and cafés start to fill*

Even in the capital, locals dine relatively early, reserving their tables for as early as 18.00, although 19.00 is more common in higher-end places. Restaurant kitchens normally close at 23.00; cafés stay open later. Many restaurants close on Monday and Tuesday, and often for a holiday in July.

Book ahead – as much as a week in advance for popular restaurants – especially for Friday and Saturday evenings. Looking to eat in one of the hottest places? You're more likely to get a reservation in the days preceding the 25th of the month, Sweden's traditional payday.

Most restaurants accept major credit cards, although smaller ones may accept only cash. Tipping is appreciated, but a service charge is factored into the bill. A 10 per cent tip is considered appropriate for good service. All bars, cafés and restaurants in Sweden are non-smoking, by law.

Entertainment & nightlife

No matter what your weaknesses are, you'll find them in Stockholm. Chill out at the Ice Bar, listen to hot jazz at Fasching or Mosebacke, dance to the latest techno at Berns, catch edgy choreography at Moderna Dansteatern, mix and mingle at Torget, party until sunrise at the wild clubs around Stureplan, or bravo a world-class tenor at the Opera House.

Stockholm may seem a bit out of the way, but the two-hour flight time to London and Paris and the rise of low-cost airlines have ensured a steady influx of influences in the way of music movements, DJs and clubbing fashion. Not that Sweden, the world's third largest music exporter, isn't setting its own trends. With countrymen like praised pop groups The Ark and The Sounds (the latter being featured on the soundtrack to TV series such as *CSI*), singer-songwriter José González, pop phenomenon The Cardigans, sprawling The Hives and electro-duo The Knife, the Swedish capital has tons to offer, with everything from exclusive and intimate concerts to full-blown rock 'n' roll spectacles.

Stureplan is the undisputable entertainment hub, its bars and clubs packed with young and glamorous party animals. Södermalm is hottest with bohemian and alternative sets, with much of the gay/lesbian scene, the rest of which is in Gamla Stan. Although things don't begin to rock until after midnight (Thursday, Friday and Saturday are the nights to prowl), arrive well before 23.00 to avoid the lines. It's not fashionably late, but you'll get in. Södermalm bars begin to close at about 01.00, clubs at 03.00, but the Stureplan scene continues as late as 05.00.

Don't expect an anything-goes attitude toward dress in otherwise live-and-let-live Stockholm. How you dress may well govern whether you are allowed in by guard-dog bouncers. Ever style-conscious, young

Swedes dress the part and you should, too, with your smartest, trendiest outfits in the Stureplan milieu, down-dressing for a more retro or boho-chic look in Södermalm. Stockholm's club scene is complicated by the strict – and perplexing – licensing laws. Permission to dance depends on authorisation to serve drinks and food, which means that many of the DJ bars do not have dance floors. Don't try to make sense of it.

The minimum drinking age is 18, but bars and clubs can set their own limits, which may be as high as 25 but are usually 23. Being smartly turned out and attractive makes you 'older', especially if you're female. Expect to pay an admission fee of SEK100–150 at the Stureplan nightclubs at weekends and as the hour grows late.

Thankfully for those who like rather more gentle evening entertainment, it's not all nightclubs and noisy bars in Stockholm. Classical music and opera fans have a ball in this city, where heavily subsidised ticket prices are among the lowest in Europe and hundreds of concerts each year are free. The music season, for both the Royal Opera and the philharmonic and symphony orchestras, extends from September to May. In summer, seek outdoor venues for concerts and music festivals.

For what's hot and happening, consult the Thursday supplement *DN På Stan* in the *Dagens Nyheter* daily newspaper or the Friday entertainment supplements in the *Aftonbladet* and *Expressen* dailies. Listings are in Swedish, but easy to interpret. More aimed at tourists is *What's on Stockholm*, available at hotels and tourist offices. Buy tickets online through individual venue websites, at Kulturhuset (see page 66), or at Sweden House in Kungsträdgården. Locals buy their tickets for opera, sports events or anything in between at the **Ticnet** website (ⓦ www.ticnet.se). Or try the Stockholm Tourist Board (see page 153), who can provide up-to-date events listings and information both in person and on their website.

Sport & relaxation

Swedes walk, jog, cycle, run, canoe, kayak, swim and work out in health clubs as a regular habit, so finding ways to get some exercise is pretty easy. And when you need to ease tired muscles, few cities offer spas like Stockholm's.

PARTICIPATION SPORTS
Walking & jogging
In Stockholm, you'll never walk alone. The abundant walking paths and promenades are well used by everyone from young parents pushing prams to senior citizens keeping fit. The same routes are good for joggers. Norr Mälarstrand skirts the water from Stadshuset (City Hall) to Rålambshov Park on Kungsholmen.

Djurgården is networked with bosky paths and waterside trails. In Haga Park, north of Norrmalm, Brunnsviken is a beautiful lake encircled by a 12 km (7½ miles) jogging trail.

Cycling
Bike paths and lanes crisscross the city, making a bicycle a good way to sightsee and to explore the wooded **Ekoparken** (ⓦ www.ekoparken.com) paths on Djurgården. Between April and October you can buy a three-day pass (SEK125) which allows you to borrow a bike from around 70 conveniently located city centre sites; passes are sold at the tourist office or online at ⓦ www.citybikes.se. The archipelago boats that carry passengers between the islands also carry cycles, making it easy to spend a day island-hopping and cycling. In summer, join a group for a guided spin around Stockholm; rates are around SEK300 for three hours and recommended companies include **Bike Hike** (ⓘ 08 649 0186 ⓦ www.bikehike.se)

from June to September and **Funky Bike Tour** (☎ 0708 544 898
ⓦ www.scanbaltexperience.com) during July to mid-August.

Paddle sports

Canoe and kayak (*kanot* and *kajak*) rentals are easy to find along
the shore, and the use of kayaks is included at some archipelago
inns, such as Grinda Wärdshus (page 135). Remember that
Stockholm's waterways are very busy with power-driven craft
and shipping that not only create huge wakes, but also may not
be able to alter their course or slow down for paddlers. Unless you
are with a guide who knows the waters and the shipping lanes,
stick close to the shore.

Golf

About 60 golf clubs are scattered around the Stockholm area, but
it's hard for visitors to play these courses unless they have local

◆ *Hole 1 on the Forest course at the Vidbynäs Golf Club*

friends who are members. To play, you must be a club member and have a green card, as well as a handicap of 36 or lower at weekends and on busy days.

Even locals are unable to play an occasional casual game at these clubs, so an alternative has sprung up: pay and play courses. Smaller than the members-only clubs and usually not so posh, they provide a low-key place for beginners or those only in town for a few days. **Vidbynäs** (❶ 08 554 90600 ❷ www.vidbynasgolf.se) is one of these, in Nykvarn. For information on other courses, visit ❷ www.golfsweden.com.

Skating

In winter, join the locals on the ice, renting skates at the rink in Kungsträdgården. You can circumnavigate the city on the ice, too, but unless you have a knowledgeable local with you, it's safer to go with a guide from Stockholm Tourist Board (see page 153). The **Stockholm Ice Skate Sailing and Touring Club** (❷ www.sssk.se) has information about routes and organised trips. It's essential to check conditions before setting foot on the ice. And never skate alone.

RELAXATION

For a workout, or to work out the kinks afterward, Stockholm offers two classy public baths. **Centralbadet** (❸ Drottninggatan 88 ❶ 08 545 21300 ❷ www.centralbadet.se) is pure turn-of-the-century eye candy, but serious about its facilities, which include a gym, saunas, steam rooms, restaurants and an amazing art nouveau swimming pool. **Sturebadet** (❸ Sturegallerian, Stureplan ❶ 08 545 01500 ❷ www.sturebadet.se), also with an art nouveau pool, is a bit more high tone, with a power-suit clientele sharing the workout room, steam rooms and pool. For those tired of the posturing of muscle-builders at the next machine, **Friskis & Svettis** (ⓐ Mäster Samuelsgatan 20 ⓣ 08 429 7000 ⓦ www.friskis.se) has all the bells and whistles, but more of a health-and-fitness mindset that appeals to the rest of us. And for the hot tub with the best view in town, check into the Clarion in Södermalm, where the top-floor spa has a reduced fee for hotel guests.

🔺 *On top of the world at the Clarion Hotel Stockholm spa*

Accommodation

Hotels in Stockholm tend toward the large and the modern, but with some notable exceptions – and with some outstanding modern hotels. Combining history and grandeur with impeccable service, the Grand Hôtel is the city's most luxurious hotel, while the Clarion in Södermalm and the sibling Clarion Hotel Sign in the centre carry the modern idea of 'art hotels' to new heights. For pure historic charm, look to Gamla Stan and the Lord Nelson and Lady Hamilton, or to the nearby luxury yacht Mälardrottningen.

Brochures on B&Bs and campsites can be downloaded from Ⓦ www.stockholmtown.com. It is a good idea to book ahead, especially in peak season. **Hotellcentralen** (Ⓦ www.hotellet.se), based in the central train station, can help with reservations.

HOTELS

Mälardrottningen ££ For mid-20th-century luxury tinged with stardust, Woolworth heiress Barbara Hutton's yacht is moored at Riddarholmen, within easy walking distance of the Royal Palace and with fine dining on board. Ⓐ On the Quay, Riddarholmen (Gamla Stan & Södermalm) Ⓣ 08 545 18780 Ⓦ www.malardrottningen.se Ⓝ T-bana: Gamla Stan

Scandic Anglais ££ If you're only in town for a weekend, this is an unbeatable location right on Stureplan. The design is fresh, modern and decidedly Nordic. See and be seen in the lobby bar and the seventh-floor, open-air terrace bar. Ⓐ Humlegårdsgatan 23 (Östermalm & Djurgården) Ⓣ 08 517 34000 Ⓦ www.scandic-hotels.com Ⓝ T-bana: Östermalmstorg

PRICE CATEGORIES

All are approximate prices for a single night in a double room/two persons during the summer season (usually with breakfast).

£ up to SEK850 ££ SEK850–1,500 £££ over SEK1,500

Story Hotel ££ This urban hotel with a twist offers smart design and arty details – perfect for guests who like their hotel room to be modern and trendy. ⓐ Riddargatan 6 (Östermalm & Djurgården) ⓘ 08 545 03940 Ⓦ www.storyhotels.com Ⓝ T-bana: Östermalmstorg

Lord Nelson Hotel ££–£££ Modern hotel with a nautical theme and cosy rooms, a half-mile from Centralstationen in the Gamla Stan area. Sauna, massage and pool are on-site. ⓐ Västerlånggatan 22 (Gamla Stan & Södermalm) ⓘ 08 506 40050 Ⓦ www.lord-nelson.se Ⓝ T-bana: Gamla Stan

Clarion Hotel Sign £££ The ultra-modern glass structure on Norra Bantorget square is one of Stockholm's most iconic buildings. Designed by Gert Wingårdh, the man behind Sweden's stunning new embassy in Washington DC, the hotel is also home to the famous New York restaurant Aquavit's first international venture. ⓐ Norra Bantorget (The centre) ⓘ 08 676 9800 Ⓦ www.clarionsign.com Ⓝ T-bana: T-Centralen

Clarion Hotel Stockholm £££ More a gallery of Scandinavian art than a hotel (ask for the illustrated guide to the collection), this luxury spot has strikingly decorated rooms and a spa with a view over Södermalm from the hot tub. ⓐ Ringvägen 98 (Gamla Stan

& Södermalm) ☎ 08 462 1000 Ⓦ www.clarionstockholm.com
Ⓝ T-bana: Skanstull

Diplomat Hotel £££ Rivalling the Grand Hôtel for heritage, sea views and pure class, the 4-star Diplomat Hotel is a safe bet for the discerning traveller. Try the T Bar for afternoon tea or a cocktail at night, when the regal ladies-who-lunch are replaced by a more party-prone crowd. ⓐ Strandvägen 7C (Östermalm & Djurgården) ☎ 08 459 6800 Ⓦ www.diplomathotel.com Ⓝ T-bana: Östermalmstorg

Grand Hôtel £££ The *grand dame* of Stockholm hotels sits across from the Royal Palace in the very centre, a bastion of grace and elegance that doesn't sacrifice warm hospitality. Dine in the Grand Veranda with views of the harbour. Large rooms combine the elegance of the past with all mod-cons. ⓐ Södra Blasieholmshamnen 8 (The centre) ☎ 08 679 3560 Ⓦ www.grandhotel.se Ⓝ T-bana: Kungsträdgården

Hotel Rival £££ Built in 1937, the former cinema Rival has been transformed into a smart, contemporary hotel with stunningly appointed rooms by its owner, ABBA impresario Benny Andersson. Well located for access to sights, it also has its own bistro, bar and bakery. All rooms have plasma TV, DVD, CD and wireless internet; parking is available. ⓐ Mariatorget 3 (Gamla Stan & Södermalm) ☎ 08 545 78910 Ⓦ www.rival.se Ⓝ T-bana: Mariatorget

Nordic Light Hotel £££ One of the city's most outstandingly modern hotels, that uses innovative lighting techniques to set the mood in its rooms. An excellent wine bar features rare American wines and the martini bar offers hundreds of options. Next to Cityterminalen's airport coaches and the Arlanda Express train. ⓐ Vasaplan 7

(The centre) ☎ 08 505 63480 ⓦ www.nordiclighthotel.se Ⓝ T-bana: T-Centralen

Nordic Sea Hotel £££ This sister to the Nordic Light is across the street, offering accommodation of the same quality, but inspired by the sea. Rooms have wireless access. The Absolut Icebar Stockholm is also here. ⓐ Vasaplan 2–4 (The centre) ☎ 08 505 63420 ⓦ www.nordicseahotel.com Ⓝ T-bana: T-Centralen

HOSTELS

Af Chapman **and Skeppsholmen £** Inexpensive sea and land hostel accommodation at two adjacent facilities. The sea rooms are aboard the striking white three-masted barque *Af Chapman* in the harbour across from the Royal Palace. It's clean, comfortable and friendly; guests are expected to clean their own rooms. Food service is available in the bar. All ages are welcome. ⓐ Flaggmansvägen 8 (The centre) ☎ 08 463 2266 ⓦ www.stfchapman.com Ⓝ T-bana: Kungsträdgården

Den Röda Båten £–££ The Red Boat once sailed the Gota Canal and the Vättern but nowadays it's one of two boats that form the hotel and hostel at the Lake Mälaren locks into the Baltic. Walk to Gamla Stan or the pubs of Södermalm. Hotel cabins have private baths. ⓐ Söder Mälarstrand 6 (Gamla Stan & Södermalm) ☎ 08 644 4385 ⓦ www.theredboat.com Ⓝ T-bana: Zinkensdamm

THE BEST OF STOCKHOLM

Whether you are on a flying visit to Stockholm or have a little more time to explore the city, its surroundings or slightly further afield, there are some sights, places and experiences that you should not miss. For the best attractions for children, see page 149.

TOP 10 ATTRACTIONS

- **Changing of the Guard** Christopher Robin would love it – all that pomp and marching to military band music (see page 102)

- **Gamla Stan** The beautiful remnants of Stockholm's medieval heritage – amid the brand new (see page 104)

- **Ferries to archipelago islands** Island dreams of peace and nature minutes away from the bustling city (see page 120)

- **Vasa Ship** Dredged from the mud and restored to reveal its full 17th-century glory (see page 92)

◆ *Bikes for hire in central Stockholm*

Suggested itineraries

HALF-DAY: STOCKHOLM IN A HURRY

If the weather is nice, wander and treat your eyes to all the sights around the watery rim of downtown Stockholm. Begin at the Royal Opera in Kungsträdgården (pick up a map at Sweden House) and follow the water past the Grand Hôtel and the white ferries and around the corner by the National Museum of Fine Arts, following the line of boats along Nybrokajen to Berzelii Park and Nybroplan. Step inside the Royal Dramatic Theatre to see the lobby, if it's open, then hop on a ferry to Djurgården to see the Vasa Ship. If you still have some time, take a ferry to Slussen and stroll through the narrow streets of Gamla Stan, browsing for a place to have lunch or dinner. Give in to the urge to stop for coffee in a cosy café or at a sidewalk table at any time.

1 DAY: TIME TO SEE A LITTLE MORE

The half-day route above makes a good beginning for a full day, leaving time to spend the afternoon in Skansen Park. The highlights not to miss there are the historic buildings, which are set along walking routes. These are arranged chronologically, so you get a mini tour of the whole country in past centuries. The mid-19th-century village has working artisans, including a baker. If this makes you hungry, you can stay in the old-time mode with a meal at **Solliden** (ⓐ Skansen Park, Djurgårdsslätten 49–51 ⓣ 08 566 37000 ⓝ Bus: 44, 47; tram 7), where they serve traditional Swedish dishes.

2–3 DAYS: TIME TO SEE MUCH MORE

While you could spend a whole day at Skansen alone, there is a great deal more to see in the city. With an extra day you can either visit

◆ Canoe around the city built on water

two or three of the many museums or begin the day in Gamla Stan, touring the Royal Palace. In that case, plan to remain for the midday Changing of the Guard. If the weather is good, you might spend the day visiting either the Viking island town of Birka (see page 65), Drottningholm Palace and its gardens, or one of the islands in the archipelago. The ride is as much the point as reaching an island. Vaxholm is the closest, but other islands are accessible on a day trip. Or take an afternoon boat to Grinda and stay overnight at Grinda Wärdshus (having made reservations, of course) and watch the sunset from their terrace before – or during – dinner (see page 135). If you have enough time, you can kayak around the island before the ferry arrives for the return trip. Or, if you return to Stockholm late in the week, it might be a good night to hit some nightspots in Stureplan.

LONGER: ENJOYING STOCKHOLM TO THE FULL

With more time, and a rented car, you could follow the route of the Gota Canal across the narrow country, stopping in Vadstena and Söderköping (see page 141) and going on to Gothenburg. Highlights there include the excellent art museum and the world's largest collection of floating museum ships, at the Maritime Centre. In the evening you might catch a show at Liseberg, or just enjoy the rides at Scandinavia's biggest amusement park.

Something for nothing

While many cities are decorated by monumental statues, few have such a continuing commitment to public art as Stockholm. And few make their most treasured museum collections of world-famous art available free to the public. This city is one big, free art gallery.

Several works by Carl Milles, Sweden's premier sculptor, adorn the city, including his *Orpheus* in front of the Concert Hall on Hötorget.

◢ *Trace Sweden's influence on building design at the Museum of Architecture*

Contemporary sculptures pop up here and there, and in the newly regenerated western edge of Södermalm, a 183 m (600 ft) long wall of colourful mosaic dresses up the buildings facing the lakeside promenade. At Kulturhuset (see page 66), you'll find free changing exhibits of art by both Swedish and international artists.

The world's longest art exhibition – more than 60 miles of it – is in the city's underground system, the Tunnelbana (or T-bana). Trains pull into nearly 100 stunning stations, each individually designed by different artists. In some, the lighting creates designs on the ceilings; others have massive, three-dimensional wall murals; others still are decorated with tiles or sculpture. Top Swedish artists began competing for these commissions as long ago as the 1950s, and the work still continues. *Art in the Stockholm Metro* is a free brochure that describes the various stations, with information on the artists. Ask at the tourist office about free guided tours of the stations. Those on the Blue Line are the most outstanding.

The National Museum of Fine Arts contains paintings by Rembrandt, Rubens, Degas and other well-known artists, as well as decorative arts from the Middle Ages to modern Swedish design treasures. Across the bridge on the island of Skeppsholmen, Moderna Museet is considered to be one of Europe's top museums of modern art. Its collections include works by Picasso and Salvador Dalí, as well as leading contemporary names. Next door is the Museum of Architecture, whose exhibit hall is chock-full of fascinating exhibits on the country's architecture, including models of buildings from all periods of its history. Excellent interactive stations offer photographs and artistic information in English.

While you're on Skeppsholmen, follow the sidewalk around its perimeter to Stockholmsbriggen. Lining the quay are dozens of historic wooden ships, some of which you can visit.

When it rains

Although Stockholm is such a beautiful city that it would be a shame to miss just strolling around and appreciating its elegant buildings and watery vistas, a rainy day does allow time to visit some of the city's museums. Along with the big – and justly famous – trio of the Vasa Ship, Nordic Museum and the National Museum of Fine Arts (any one of which can easily take half a day to peruse at leisure), a rainy day gives travellers the perfect excuse to explore some little-known treasures. Among these is the Army Museum, with exhibitions on everything from the secret world of spies to weird medieval weapons. The musically inclined will enjoy the Music Museum, with its collections of old instruments and enough hands-on toys to keep even an adult occupied. The various museums inside the Royal Palace make a good rainy-day choice, too, since they are concentrated closely together. The various state apartments, the Treasury and a museum that explores the origins of the earlier fortress are all within the palace complex. And a good selection of restaurants is only a few (wet) steps away.

Another occupation for a rainy day is shopping in one of the covered complexes. For high end, visit Nordiska Kompaniet (NK), no longer a true department store but a series of label shops run by top brands. Below Sergels Torg is an underground shopping street, including a branch of DesignTorget. Choose the upscale Sturegallerian mall in Stureplan and you can even top off your shopping with a sauna, massage or swim at Sturebadet spa and health club. And any place with more than five or six shops is bound to have a café, where you can join locals at their most cherished custom, the coffee break.

● *Explore Sweden through the fascinating exhibits at the Nordic Museum*

On arrival

TIME DIFFERENCE
Sweden follows Central European Time (CET). During Daylight Saving Time (late March to late September), the clocks are put forward by one hour.

ARRIVING
By air
Most international flights arrive at **Arlanda Airport** (📞 08 797 6000 🌐 www.lfv.se), north of Stockholm. **Flygbussarna** coaches (📞 08 588 22828 🌐 www.flygbussarna.se) depart every 10–15 minutes, taking 40 minutes to reach the Cityterminalen. A one-way trip costs SEK110, with a return costing SEK199. Alternatively, **Arlanda Express** trains (📞 020 222 224 🌐 www.arlandaexpress.com) leave every 10–15 minutes and take 20 minutes to reach Centralstationen. A one-way fare is SEK240 (SEK120 if you're under 26) and a return costs SEK460 – travellers on a budget should note that this is almost double the price of the Flygbussarna. Taxis can take you to the door of your hotel, but cost about SEK450–500. The major companies have fixed rates, and if you pre-book before arrival, you won't have to stand in a queue. Contact **Taxi Stockholm** (📞 08 150 000) or **Taxi Kurir** (📞 08 300 000).

   Bromma Airport (📞 08 797 6800 🌐 www.lfv.se), about 8 km (5 miles) west of Stockholm, handles domestic and some international flights, mostly to business destinations such as Brussels. About 100 km (62 miles) south of the city, near Nyköping, is **Skavsta Airport** (📞 0155 28 0400 🌐 www.skavsta-air.se), handling both domestic and international flights, mostly by low-cost carriers. Flygbussarna coaches (see opposite) to Cityterminalen from

Bromma (SEK69 one way) and Skavsta (SEK130) are linked to flight schedules.

By rail
Trains from Arlanda airport, Gothenburg and Malmö, as well as Denmark and Oslo, arrive at **Centralstationen** (ⓐ Centralplan 1 ☎ 0771 757 575) which is centrally located in Norrmalm. It has all the usual facilities including a police station and lost property office, and links to the T-bana system.

By road
Buses from both airports and from all over Sweden and Europe (Bucharest, Sarajevo, Belgrade, Copenhagen, Oslo) arrive at **Cityterminalen** (ⓐ Klarabergsviadukten 72 ☎ 08 762 5997 ⓦ www.cityterminalen.com), the city's main bus station located near the railway station. It is a short walk to the nearest T-bana stop and there are plenty of bus connections and taxis here too.

While the city is easier to drive in than most European capitals, a car is more of a liability than an asset. Traffic is not heavy, partly because locals don't see much point in paying for fuel and parking – both expensive – when public transport is so good and safe. If you do drive in the city, expect delays on the bridges between its various islands. Parking is either in multi-level car parks or on-street. Machines that provide tickets for street parking accept coins or credit/debit cards.

Drink-driving spot checks are very frequent. If you are caught driving after drinking just a little less than one glass of beer, you will be prosecuted. Speed limits and other rules of the road are explained on the website of the **Swedish Road Administration** (ⓦ www.vv.se).

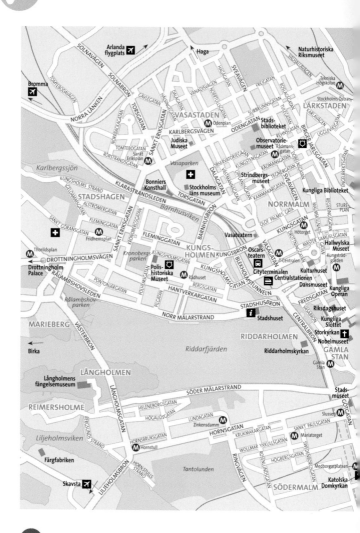

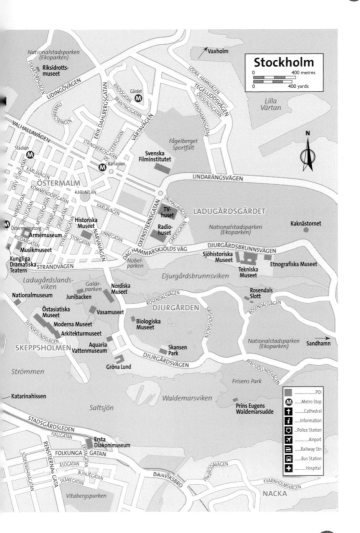

By water

Stockholm has a number of ports which service ferry terminals, cruise ships or boat services around the archipelago (see page 120). Many are close to the city centre; those further out usually have public transport connections to the centre of town to cater for arriving vessels. The largest company is **Strömma Kanalbolaget** (❶ 08 587 14000 ⓦ www.strommakanalbolaget.se), with services to Drottningholm Palace, Birka, Vaxholm, Sandhamn and other popular destinations. Its one-day Thousand Islands sightseeing cruise (including lunch and a two-course dinner) is highly recommended.

FINDING YOUR FEET

Central Stockholm was designed to be viewed across water. Some of its most striking buildings sit facing the lake or harbours, so admire them full face, in an uninterrupted view. Everything is sparkling clean and tidy, heightened on a clear summer's day by the incomparable northern light that has inspired so many artists, and at night by the myriad lights doubled by the water's reflection.

The city is also safe. Even its underground system is bright and virtually crime-free. Drivers are normally careful of pedestrians. The greatest risk is in assuming pedestrians have the right of way when crossing bicycle lanes. Whatever the law may be, cyclists do not willingly stop for those on foot, and consider their lanes sacred. Cross with extreme caution.

ORIENTATION

Although its setting on a series of islands means that Stockholm has no overall plan of grid streets and arteries, it is not difficult to find your way. Each section is named; those you will spend the most time in are Norrmalm and Östermalm (side by side on the 'mainland') and

IF YOU GET LOST, TRY ...

Excuse me, do you speak English?
Ursäkta mig, talar du engelska?
Ew-shekta mey, tahlar doo eng-ehl-ska?

How do I get to ...?
Hur kommer man till ...?
Huhr kommehr mahn til ...?

Can you show me on my map?
Kan du visa mig på kartan?
Kahn duh visah mey poh kahrtahn?

the islands of Gamla Stan, Skeppsholmen and Djurgården. The latter two are almost exclusively made up of museums, and Gamla Stan is easily recognised by the Royal Palace crowning its hill. For nightlife, you will want to cross through Gamla Stan's cobbled streets to Södermalm, or head for downtown Stureplan, bordering on Östermalm.

Stockholm is a supremely walkable city, with boats shuttling back and forth between many of the islands to shorten the distances. A sightseeing tour by boat will help you get a sense of where everything lies and recognise some of the landmarks: the City Hall, the Royal Palace, Parliament, Riddarholmen Church, the Royal Dramatic Theatre, Slussen, Grand Hôtel and the Globe Arena.

GETTING AROUND

The modern, fast and safe Tunnelbana (T-bana) system covers the entire city, except for Skeppsholmen and Djurgården. These can be reached by buses 65 and 44 plus 47, respectively, and Djurgården can also be accessed by the vintage tram 7 from Norrmalmstorg. Incidentally, this old tram line is great fun to ride even if it's not particularly efficient; check the website of the **Swedish Tramway Society** (W www.sparvagssallskapet.se) for more information.

Public transport in Stockholm is run by **SL** (T 08 600 1000 W www.sl.se). You can buy T-bana and bus tickets at SL centres or from ticket agents which display the SL logo. Single tickets are valid for one hour and range from SEK40 to SEK80 according to how many zones you need to travel in. Remember to validate the ticket as you enter the T-bana or bus. You can also buy a pass which allows you unlimited transit for 24 hours (SEK100), 72 hours (SEK200), or seven days (SEK260).

The most scenic route for hopping between the museum islands and Gamla Stan or Nybroplan is via the little walk-on ferries that shuttle back and forth. The route from Gamla Stan operates year-round; the others are seasonal. Boats heading to Drottningholm Palace, Birka and other points in the western archipelago leave from Stadshuset (City Hall). A handy hop-on, hop-off tour is offered by **Stockholm Sightseeing** (T 08 1200 4000 W www.stockholmsightseeing.com), with commentary and stops at the five major areas of attractions. Tickets cost SEK100 for 24 hours and offer additional discounts on entrance fees to certain attractions.

Ferries connect the major islands of the archipelago, most leaving from Strandvägen. **Cinderella Boats** (T 08 120 04000 W www.cinderellabatarna.com) operate several trips each day to Vaxholm, Grinda, Sandhamn and several others. A five-day archipelago pass, available at the tourist office in Sweden House, allows unlimited boat travel among the islands.

The Stockholm Card provides unlimited transport on the

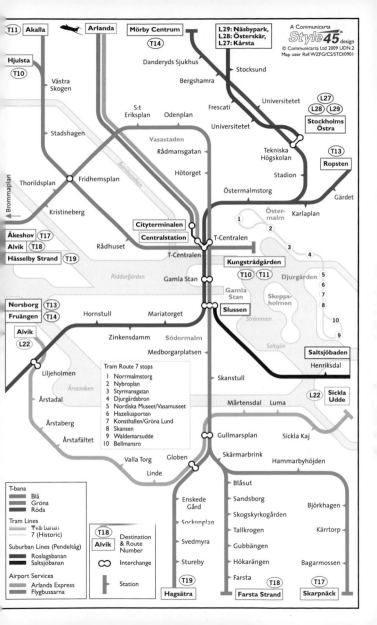

T-bana, buses and some ferries, free access to 75 museums and sights, plus two boat tours and discounts on other tours. The card costs SEK375 for 24 hours, SEK495 for 48 hours and SEK595 for 72 hours, and is available from the tourist office.

Reliable taxi companies are **Taxi Stockholm** (☎ 08 150 000), **Taxi Kurir** (☎ 08 300 000) and **Taxi 020** (☎ 020 20 20 20), clearly identified by their signs. Apart from airport transfers, taxis are usually metered, starting at about SEK45.

CAR HIRE

All major companies are represented in Stockholm, most with desks at Arlanda Airport. **Europcar** (☎ 08 462 4800 ⓦ www.europcar.com) is a popular car rental company in Stockholm, offering competitive rates.

If you plan to stay in the city before travelling elsewhere, consider picking up the car as you leave Stockholm. This saves driving in the city and paying for parking. The minimum age for car hire is 18, and you must present (and carry while driving) your driving licence. You will also need to produce a credit card, even if you are not charging the car to it.

Before leaving the car park, be sure you have all documents and that you know how to operate the vehicle. The most immediate problem is for those from left-hand-drive countries. Not only are you driving on the opposite side of the road, but you must operate the gears with the wrong hand. Take care on roundabouts or on dual-lane highways, it's easy to make mistakes.

● *The iconic Stadshuset – Stockholm's City Hall*

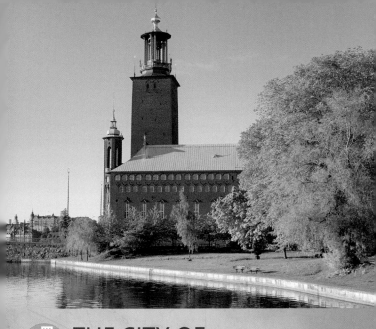

THE CITY OF
Stockholm

The centre

Norrmalm is the heart of modern downtown Stockholm, where shops, offices, clubs and theatres share elegant streets with grand hotels, smart restaurants and cafés. It is the city's transportation hub, too, with Centralstationen, Cityterminalen and T-Centralen together in its middle. The almost-round island of Skeppsholmen hangs out into the harbour, tethered by a single bridge. More bridges lead west to Kungsholmen, and to the north the downtown streets and avenues continue into Vasastaden.

SIGHTS & ATTRACTIONS

Just walking along the streets in the area that locals call simply 'City', with its busy harbours, tidy gardens and variety of architecture, is interesting. Expect plenty of subjects to aim your camera toward.

Boats to Drottningholm & Birka

The dock just in front of Stadshuset (City Hall) is the boarding place for boats to Drottningholm Palace (see page 68) and to the Viking site at Birka (see page 65). Boats leave for the palace at hourly intervals between May and October, costing SEK150 for a return ticket or SEK270 for a combined boat and palace entry ticket. Boats to Birka leave at 09.30 between May and August, and again at 13.00 between June and August, with the SEK265 return ticket including the entrance fee and guides. For detailed timetables, see Ⓦ www.strommakanalbolaget.se.

Centralbadet

An outstanding art nouveau building from 1904 by architect Wilhelm Klemming, the interior and courtyard are worth visiting,

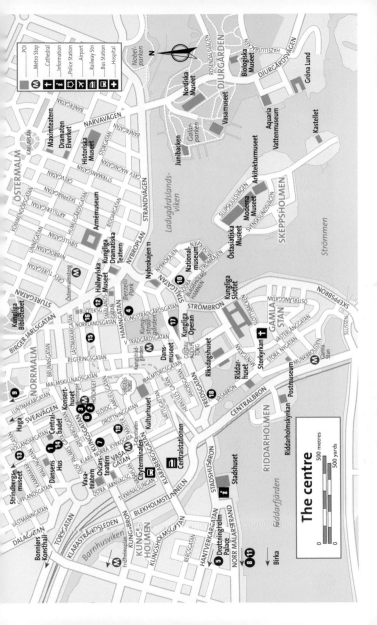

The centre

····	POI
Ⓜ	Metro Stop
✝	Cathedral
𝒊	Information
✈	Airport
🚉	Railway Stn
🚌	Bus Station
✚	Hospital

0   500 metres
0   500 yards

even if you don't plan to use its spa or swimming facilities. The interior is beautifully preserved, with stained glass, stenciling, ornamental metal work and other details in classic art nouveau designs. The exterior, facing onto the courtyard, also has excellent architectural details and a quiet garden. ⓐ Drottninggatan 88 ❶ 08 545 21300 ⓦ www.centralbadet.se ⓛ 06.00–22.00 Mon–Fri, 08.00–20.00 Sat, 08.00–17.00 Sun; closed Sun, July & Aug (opening hours change frequently, check website) Ⓝ T-bana: Hötorget

Haga

The rolling green fields inspired by English landscape gardening in the 19th century have lost none of their charm. Perfect for romantic walks under avenues of stately trees or picnics on softly formed lawns and open meadows. The many historic buildings, such as the Copper Tent from 1787, the Haga Palace where the present King of Sweden grew up, the Turkish Pavilion and the butterfly museum, set the mind in motion. Dream away to past times, and enjoy nature's unspoilt beauty. ⓐ Hagaparken, Solna Ⓝ Bus: 40, 59, 70, 515, 176/177

Harbours

With boats and ships constantly moving throughout its waterways, the whole city is a harbour, but the busiest sections surround the point of land between Nybroplan, Slussen, Stadshuset (City Hall) and Kungsträdgården. Ferries, sightseeing boats, floating restaurants and café boats dock here, relieving the formality of the surrounding buildings with their bobbing confusion of colours and shapes. The harbours are always inspiring places to sit and watch the world glide by.

◐ *Art nouveau splendour at the swimming baths – Centralbadet*

Historic ships

Docked along the eastern shore of the small island of Skeppsholmen are dozens of historic vessels, most privately owned and a few offering sailing experiences to the public. A sidewalk runs the length of this area, which was once a busy shipyard, ending at the dock for the ferry to Djurgården. The ferry is a much faster route than going by land around Nybroplan.

Hötorget

The square north of Sergels Torg is enclosed by larger-than-life buildings that seem to dwarf it. One side is occupied by the PUB department store, another by the columned façade of the Stockholms Konserthus (Concert Hall). This 1926 building is one of the city's few in the art deco style. In the square is an outdoor market with fresh produce and flowers. Here, too, is Hötorgshallen, a food market hall, a bit less toney (and pricey) than Saluhallen at Östermalmstorg.

Stadshuset (City Hall)

Perhaps Scandinavia's best-known building, the brick Stadshuset seems to rise directly from the water at the end of Kungsholmen. The best view of it is from the island of Riddarholmen, beyond the Riddarholmskyrkan (Riddarholm Church). The courtyard is open to the public, but the Golden Hall and Blue Hall, where the Nobel prizes are awarded by the King each December, can only be seen on a guided tour (offered in English every day, all year round). The Golden Hall depicts scenes from Swedish history in a gold-leaf mosaic of over 18 million pieces. Climb the tower, just shy of 106 m (350 ft) tall, for views across the city. ➌ Hantverkargatan 1 ➊ 08 508 29059

▶ *Hötorget's big, bold architecture reaches up into Stockholm's clear skies*

🕐 10.00–16.00 May–Sept; tours in English: 10.00, 12.00 Ⓝ T-bana: T-Centralen, Rådhuset. Admission charge

CULTURE

Tiny Skeppsholmen island, connected to Norrmalm by a bridge from the end of Strömkajen (by the National Museum of Fine Arts), has a surprisingly high concentration of museums, including the Museum of Modern Art.

Arkitekturmuseet (Museum of Architecture)

This small but fascinating display hall shows models and photographs of Swedish architectural styles from the earliest time through to the present. These are supplemented by excellent interpretive material in English, so you can explore any style and not only learn more about it but find existing examples in Stockholm. The shop is equally outstanding: a complete bookshop of art and design books in most languages, with a good selection of gifts. ⓐ Skeppsholmen ☏ 08 5872 7000 Ⓦ www.arkitekturmuseet.se 🕐 10.00–20.00 Tues, 10.00–18.00 Wed–Sun Ⓝ T-bana: Kungsträdgården. Admission charge; free Fri

Bonniers Konsthall

This major new venue for contemporary Swedish and international art was founded in 2006 by art patron Jeanette Bonnier, whose family runs a Scandinavian publishing empire through the Bonnier Group. But this is no grand, stuffy building; it's beautifully light and airy, with a soft triangular shape. According to the architects, it reflects a desire for openness to the changing modes of expression in the world of contemporary art. ⓐ Torsgatan 19 ☏ 08 736 4248

BIRKA

Between AD750 and 1050, a Viking settlement flourished on the island of Birka, west of Stockholm, and the ramparts on the hilltop there, are the only monumental remains of the Viking world that exist anywhere. This, and the rich finds in more than 1,600 grave mounds have made this a UNESCO World Heritage Site. Birka was a trade centre, with rich merchants from Belgium, Holland and France sailing into Lake Mälaren to trade goods from Europe and the Islamic world for fur, and for the fine metalwork for which the Vikings were known. Today archaeologists still seek to know more about the culture and life of these people, as they interpret the finds in the graves and village. Excellent tours of the island are led by these archaeologists, who paint a vivid picture of how the island once looked. A museum illustrates Viking life with models of houses and boats, along with displays of items found in the site and in graves. The small gift shop is a good source of books on the Vikings, as well as reproductions of their jewellery and other artefacts. Sweden's largest fleet of Viking ship replicas anchors here, with a shipyard, working blacksmith, sail weavers and other craftsmen working to outfit and repair the ships. For transport here, see page 58.

Ⓦ www.bonnierskonsthall.se Ⓛ 11.00–20.00 Wed, 11.00–17.00 Thur–Sun Ⓝ T-bana: St Eriksplan. Admission charge

Dansmuseet (Museum of Dance)

The collections of this interesting museum relate to dance through the ages and around the world, showing everything from African masks to costumes from the Parisian, Russian and Swedish ballets of the 1910s and 1920s. Watch dance videos, see live lunchtime performances or learn tango and African dancing at seasonal classes. 📍 Gustav Adolfs Torg 22–24 ☎ 08 441 7650 🌐 www.dansmuseet.se 🕐 11.00–16.00 Mon–Fri, 12.00–16.00 Sat & Sun, May–Sept; 11.00–16.00 Tues–Fri, 12.00–16.00 Sat & Sun, Oct–Apr Ⓜ T-bana: Kungsträdgården. Admission charge for exhibitions

Hallwylska Museet (Hallwyl Palace)

Hallwyl Palace, facing Berzelii Park, dates from the late 19th century, and its sumptuous rooms have remained unaltered since the 1920s, when it was still the private residence of the von Hallwyl family. You can step inside to admire the courtyard, staircases and foyer and to browse the shop, or pay to see the next floor unescorted. The rest of the palatial home is open for a guided tour (in English, 13.00 Sundays). Designed by the architect of the Nordic Museum, Isak Gustaf Clason, it was the marvel of modernity in its day – the first home in Stockholm with running water, electricity, central heating and telephones, plus one of the first bathrooms in Sweden. Interestingly, Countess Wilhelmina von Hallwyl had always intended for her home to be turned into a museum, and thus made sure to save everything – from priceless art to everyday objects such as silver-plated hairbrushes. 📍 Hamngatan 4 ☎ 08 402 3099 🌐 www.hallwylskamuseet.se 🕐 11.45–16.00 Tues, Thur & Fri, 11.45–16.00, 17.45–19.00 Wed, 11.30–16.00 Sat & Sun Ⓜ T-bana: Östermalmstorg. Admission charge

Kulturhuset

A cultural hub that was once the inspiration for the Centre Pompidou in Paris. With exhibitions of national and international artists, performances, debates and lectures, Stockholm's House

⬥ *Culture hub, Kulturhuset, on Sergels Torg*

DROTTNINGHOLM PALACE

Modelled after Versailles, but much more inviting and far less pompous, Drottningholm Palace is the residence of the Swedish Royal Family. The palace was constructed in the late 1600s, with a second storey added to the wings in the following century. Drottningholms Slottsteater (the Court Theatre), the pavilion of Kina Slott and the English Park and French formal gardens were also added in the 1700s. The entire ensemble was declared a UNESCO World Heritage Site in 1991.

On a tour of the palace interior (with a guide or independently with a descriptive brochure) you can see the rooms designed by Nicodemus Tessin the Elder, Sweden's foremost early baroque architect. These include the magnificent grand staircase, the Ehrenstrahl Drawing Room and the dowager Queen's State Bedchamber. Karl XI's gallery and the elegant library date from later work.
❶ 08 402 6280 **Ⓦ** www.royalcourt.se **❶** 10.00–16.30 May–Aug; 12.00–15.30 Sept; 12.00–15.30 Sat & Sun, Oct–Apr
Ⓝ T-bana: Brommaplan. Admission charge

Drottningholm Court Theatre

Completed in 1766, the Drottningholms Slottsteater is much like a stage set itself, its décor worked in papier mâché, stucco and paint. The original Italian stage machinery allows quick scene changes and provides such special effects as moving waves and clouds, wind and thunder. One of only a handful of early European theatres remaining, this one is especially rare for having its original 18th-century stage sets (which have been copied for use in performances) and machinery in good working order. Productions often feature lesser-known operas, focusing largely on French baroque opera. Half-hourly guided tours include a look into this backstage bag of tricks. ❶ 08 660 8225; tickets 0771 707 070 ⓦ www.dtm.se ❸ Tickets: 11.00–12.00, 14.00–15.00 Mon–Fri; tours: 11.00–16.30 May–Aug; 13.00–15.30 Sept. Admission charge

Kina Slott
A birthday gift for a queen, this pleasure palace, in the form of a red and yellow 'Chinese' pavilion, has curving wings and decorations in a theme inspired by 18th-century notions of China. ❶ 08 402 6270 ⓦ www.royalcourt.se ❸ 11.00–16.30, May–Aug; 12.00–15.30 Sept. Admission charge

of Culture really does have something for everyone. The bookstore Konst-ig offers literature on art and design, and Lava youth centre keeps young teenagers busy while you check up on what's happening in your home town at the World News Café. Don't miss Stockholmsterrassen, a 700 sq m roof terrace for coffee and clubbing (only open in summer). ❷ Sergels Torg 3 ❶ 08 506 31508 ⓦ www.kulturhuset.se ❸ Hours vary; check website ❷ T-bana: T-Centralen

Kungliga Operan (Royal Opera House)
Elegant and showy enough to contradict the Swedish *lagom* ('no more than is necessary') fetish, this hallowed shrine of the high C has a gold-

plated lobby nearly 30 m (100 ft) wide, its ceiling dripping with crystal chandeliers. Jenny Lind, the Swedish Nightingale, began her career here. It houses three restaurants; the Operabaren has a masterpiece *Jugendstil* (art nouveau) interior, worth the price of lunch just to revel in. ⓐ Gustav Adolfs Torg ⓣ 08 791 4400 ⓦ www.operan.se ⓝ T-bana: Kungsträdgården

Moderna Museet (Museum of Modern Art)

The entire 20th century to the present is represented, in more than 5,000 paintings, sculptures and installations, 25,000 watercolours, drawings and graphics, and around 100,000 photographs by artists including Matisse, Picasso, Klee and Dalí. It is one of Europe's major modern art collections. The light, modern building also includes an espresso bar, restaurant and a shop selling jewellery, home accessories, art books and prints. ⓐ Skeppsholmen ⓣ 08 519 55200 ⓦ www.modernamuseet.se ⓛ 10.00–20.00 Tues, 10.00–18.00 Wed–Sun ⓝ T-bana: Kungsträdgården. Admission charge

Nationalmuseum (National Museum of Fine Arts)

The more than 16,000 paintings and sculptures represent all schools and styles from the Middle Ages through to the early 20th century, with works by Rembrandt, Rubens, Renoir, Goya, Degas and Gauguin as well as those of the foremost Nordic artists. The 18th-century French collection is especially renowned for its size and quality. Applied arts and design collections are strongest in ceramic art (more than a third of the 30,000 pieces), but contain good glass, textiles, furniture and metal arts. The museum's magnificent murals were painted by Sweden's most famous artist, Carl Larsson; on the top floor is his powerful 6 by 14 m (20 by 46 ft) oil painting *Midwinter Sacrifice* (1915). ⓐ Södra Blasieholmshamnen ⓣ 08 519 54300

🌐 www.nationalmuseum.se 🕐 11.00–20.00 Tues, 11.00–17.00
Wed–Sun Ⓝ T-bana: Kungsträdgården. Admission charge

Strindbergsmuseet (Strindberg Museum)

August Strindberg, the fiery, tormented author of plays such as *Miss Julie* and *The Dance of Death*, is – together with Norwegian playwright Henrik Ibsen – seen as one of the founders of modern naturalistic theatre. His preserved home in central Stockholm (three rooms, no kitchen) is a journey back in time. The street that leads up to the museum has familiar Strindberg *bon mots* inscribed in the street cement with golden letters. And in Tegnérlunden, the small park next to the museum, a giant statue of the master has been raised. The conditions for a veritable Strindberg Walk are, in other words, perfect.
ⓐ Drottninggatan 85 ☎ 08 411 5354 🌐 www.strindbergsmuseet.se
🕐 12.00–16.00 Tues–Sun Sept–June; 10.00–16.00 Tues–Sun, July
& Aug Ⓝ T-bana: Rådmansgatan, Odenplan

RETAIL THERAPY

The city's premier department stores are in Norrmalm, along with street after street of shops and underground galleries lined with even more. Kungsholmen is an up-and-coming neighbourhood for shopping, less pricey and a bit less predictable.

Åhléns City For trendy fashion – both Swedish and international – or a little something to decorate your flat with, this department store has it. Music and food share the lower level. The day spa is pure luxury.
ⓐ Klarabergsgatan 50 ☎ 08 676 6000 🌐 www.ahlens.com
🕐 10.00–20.00 Mon–Fri, 10.00–19.00 Sat, 11.00–18.00 Sun
Ⓝ T-bana: T-Centralen

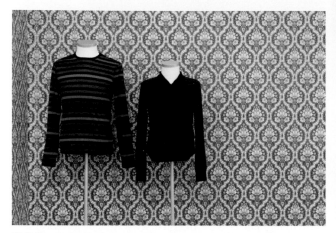

● *Åhléns City has the latest Swedish and international designer fashions*

DesignTorget Be the first to see and buy what's new and cool by the hottest designers and by students who haven't yet made their name. You may find anything from fridge magnets to furniture here, but it will always be fresh and clever. Also on Södermalm's main street Götgatan, in Östermalm mall Fältöversten, Kungsholmen's Västermalmsgallerian and on Nybrogatan 16, behind the Royal Dramatic Theatre. ⓐ Kulturhuset (lower level), Sergels Torg ⓣ 08 219 150 ⓦ www.designtorget.se ⓛ 10.00–19.00 Mon–Fri, 10.00–18.00 Sat, 11.00–17.00 Sun ⓝ T-bana: T-Centralen

Gallerian A fresh, funky shopping centre filled with brands such as Puma Concept, Topshop and H&M, as well as the mini-spa Axelsons. ⓐ Hamngatan 37 ⓣ 08 791 2445 ⓦ www.gallerian.se ⓛ 10.00–19.00 Mon–Fri, 10.00–18.00 Sat, 11.00–17.00 Sun ⓝ T-bana: T-Centralen

The Grandpa Designed to look like a '1970s French Riviera hotel', this ultra-trendy, two-tiered lifestyle store is probably not your grandpa's cup of tea. Dresses are hung on luggage rails, there are blow-dryers in the changing rooms, and you pay for your chic finds at the concierge's desk. It's located slightly out of the centre: to get there, follow Kungsbron to Fleminggatan, which crosses Fridhemsgatan. ⓐ Fridhemsgatan 43 ⓣ 08 643 6081 ⓦ www.grandpa.se ⓛ 11.00–19.00 Mon–Fri, 11.00–17.00 Sat, 12.00–16.00 Sun ⓝ T-bana: Fridhemsplan

Hötorgshallen Food purveyors sell imported goodies and local ingredients in a busy market setting. Sample delicacies from around the world. ⓐ Hötorget ⓣ 08 230 001 ⓦ www.hotorgshallen.se ⓛ 10.00–18.00 Mon–Thur, 10.00–18.30 Fri, 10.00–16.00 Sat ⓝ T-bana: Hötorget

NK (Nordiska Kompaniet) Five storeys of haute everything, richly displayed in a *Jugendstil* building, NK is a destination and an attraction as much as a shopping experience. Ladies – and not a few men – lunch on the top floor, and the lower floor is a food emporium. For all its grandeur, it's not intimidating to shop here. ⓐ Hamngatan 18–20 ⓣ 08 762 8000 ⓦ www.nk.se ⓛ 10.00–20.00 Mon–Fri, 10.00–18.00 Sat, 12.00–17.00 Sun ⓝ T-bana: T-Centralen

Stockhome Everything your Euro-chic living space needs, in sleek modern designs. Refurnish your kitchen with glassware and dishes, choose cool new towels, or redo the nursery. If they're clever enough to come up with the perfect name for the store, you can trust their choice of stuff to fill it with. ⓐ Kungsgatan 25 ⓣ 08 230 800 ⓦ www.stockhome.se ⓛ 10.00–19.00 Mon–Fri, 10.00–17.00 Sat, 12.00–17.00 Sun ⓝ T-bana: Hötorget

TAKING A BREAK

Cafés are a local institution, places to indulge in the national pastime of drinking coffee and chatting with friends. The posher ones serve sumptuous teacakes and pastries. When you need a respite from shopping and sightseeing, this part of town offers the ultimate old-fashioned spa with a café and garden, as well as waterside parks for quiet repose.

Centralbadet £ ❶ Full of character and serving fresh, healthy lunches and snacks, this glorious art nouveau bath house has its original 1904 interior of stained-glass panels and stencilled walls. Munch your grilled focaccio or fresh fruit salad at café tables in or out in the secluded garden. You may be tempted to take a longer break and spend the afternoon relaxing in the spa. ⓐ Drottninggatan 88 ❶ 08 545 21300 Ⓦ www.centralbadet.se ⓛ 06.00–20.30 Mon–Fri, 08.00–20.30 Sat, 08.00–17.30 Sun ⓝ T-bana: Hötorget

Hurry Curry £ ❷ Tempting scents of curry, cardamom and saffron draw the crowds to this Indian tea salon right by Hötorget square. Buy the house cutlery or plates from aligning shop, Indiska. ⓐ Slöjdgatan 11 ❶ 08 233 080 Ⓦ www.hurrycurry.se ⓛ 10.00–20.00 Mon–Sat ⓝ T-bana: Hötorget

Kungshallen £ ❸ Apart from the usual hamburger chains, Kungshallen food hall is one of very few budget food options in the centre. Each weekday, around 9,000 guests crowd the 15 restaurants, which range from Thai, Japanese and Lebanese to classic Swedish fare. ⓐ Kungsgatan 44 ❶ 08 218 005 Ⓦ www.kungshallen.nu ⓛ 09.00–23.00 Mon–Fri, 11.00–23.00 Sat, 12.00–23.00 Sun ⓝ T-bana: Hötorget

Max £ ❹ If you have a hunger that only a burger can fill, head for the nearest branch of Sweden's oldest fast-food chain for a Maxburger or a Max Deluxe. ❷ Kungsträdgårdsgatan 20 ❶ 08 611 3810 Ⓦ www.max.se ❶ 10.00–05.00 Sun–Thur, 10.00–06.00 Fri & Sat ❷ T-bana: Kungsträdgården

Muffin Bakery £ ❺ Muffins aren't the only tasty things here: warm soups, salads and sandwiches are on the menu, too. To reach it, follow Kungsbron to Fleminggatan, which crosses Fridhemsgatan. ❷ Fridhemsgatan 3 ❶ 08 651 8800 Ⓦ www.muffinbakery.se ❶ 09.00–20.00 Mon–Thur, 09.00–18.00 Sat & Sun ❷ T-bana: Fridhemsplan

Publik £ ❻ The fashionable café and restaurant on the third floor of trendy department store PUB makes for the perfect pit stop during a shopping spree in the city. ❷ PUB, Hötorget, off Kungsgatan or Drottninggatan ❶ 08 518 0410 Ⓦ www.publik03.se ❶ 08.00–19.00 Mon–Fri, 10.00–18.00 Sat, 11.00–17.00 Sun ❷ T-bana: T-Centralen, Hötorget

Vete-Katten £ ❼ Very old-school European, in the grand manner, Vetekatten overlooks the park and is the genteel choice for coffee and a little something. ❷ Kungsgatan 55 ❶ 08 208 405 Ⓦ www.vetekatten.se ❶ 07.30–19.00 Mon–Fri, 09.30–17.00 Sat, 12.00–17.00 Sun ❷ T-bana: Hötorget

Mälarpaviljongen ££ ❽ If the day is fine, take your coffee alfresco and watch the boats go by. After the shops close, this is a popular place to watch the sun set with an aquavit. They serve food as well. ❷ Norr Mälarstrand 64 ❶ 08 650 8701 Ⓦ www.malarpaviljongen.se ❶ 11.00–late; times vary according to weather ❷ T-bana: Fridhemsplan

Republik ££ ❾ The cosy interior of this French/Swedish bar, café and brasserie features black wooden panels and red medallion wallpaper. In summer, head for the open-air terrace out back. ⓐ Tulegatan 17 ⓣ 08 545 905 50 ⓦ www.restaurant-republik.com ⓛ 11.00–00.00 Mon–Thur, 17.00–00.00 Fri & Sat ⓣ T-bana: Rådmansgatan

Cadierbaren at Grand Hôtel ££–£££ ❿ A timeless lounge with picturesque views. Stop by for expertly shaken cocktails, sumptuous afternoon teas or simply a slice of the refined Grand Hôtel atmosphere. If you're looking to have dinner, famous Swedish chef Mathias Dahlgren, from Michelin-awarded restaurant Bon Lloc, has a restaurant here. With renowned skills and a menu that changes according to seasons, this new hotspot is almost guaranteed success. ⓐ Södra Blasieholmshamnen 8 ⓣ 08 679 3585 ⓦ www.grandhotel.se ⓛ 07.00–02.00 Mon–Fri, 08.00–02.00 Sat, 08.00–01.00 Sun ⓣ T-bana: Kungsträdgården

AFTER DARK

As the offices and shops begin to close, the bars come alive. That scene segues into dinner and then – on Thursday, Friday and Saturday nights – to the clubs. Things don't really pick up clubwise until after midnight. While not as haute-brow as neighbouring Stureplan, Norrmalm is decidedly not the place to dress down.

RESTAURANTS

Kungsholmen £–££ ⓫ The most affordable amongst the restaurants of the F12 Group, which also runs the excellent Fredsgatan 12, Grill and Restaurangen. The place is displayed as a large food court set beautifully on the waterfront near City Hall, and serves anything from sushi to Scandinavian cuisine. ⓐ Norr Mälarstrand, Kajplats 464

☎ 08 505 24450 **Ⓦ** www.kungsholmen.com **🕐** 17.00–01.00 Mon–Sat, 12.00–19.00 Sun **Ⓝ** T-bana: Fridhemsplan

KB Restaurant and Bar ££ ⑫ Join the arts set at their favourite hangout for several generations. The food is classic Swedish cooking – not always easy to find in trendy Stockholm – and always good. Look up at the highly theatrical art nouveau façade before you enter. **ⓐ** Smålandsgatan 7 **☎** 08 679 6032 **Ⓦ** www.konstnarsbaren.se **🕐** 11.30–00.00 Mon–Fri, 13.00–00.00 Sat, 13.00–22.00 Sun **Ⓝ** T-bana: Östermalmstorg

Tranan ££ ⑬ An institution in Stockholm, serving hearty, traditional Swedish classics since 1929. Below the restaurant is a bar with a mixed after-work clientele and a nice vibe. **ⓐ** Karlbergsvägen 14 **☎** 08 527 28100 **Ⓦ** www.tranan.se **🕐** 17.00–00.00 Mon–Sat, 17.00–23.00 Sun **Ⓝ** T-bana: Odenplan

Grill ££–£££ ⑭ Choose between five different menus inspired by five different continents in this grill restaurant. Dining rooms are themed: eat in Versailles, South Beach Miami, or a hunting cabin. **ⓐ** Drottninggatan 89 **☎** 08 314 530 **Ⓦ** www.grill.se **🕐** 11.30–14.00, 17.00–01.00 Mon–Fri, 17.00–01.00 Sat, 15.00–23.00 Sun **Ⓝ** T-bana: Odenplan

Prinsen ££–£££ ⑮ Art and artists are central themes, the walls covered in paintings and the booths filled with writers and artists. Dine on traditional dishes, especially the herring, along with some more avant-garde choices. **ⓐ** Mäster Samuelsgatan 4 **☎** 08 611 1331 **Ⓦ** www.restaurangprinsen.com **🕐** 11.30 23.30 Mon–Fri, 13.00–23.30 Sat, 17.00–22.30 Sun **Ⓝ** T-bana: Östermalmstorg

Zink Grill ££–£££ ⑯ A charming restaurant serving breakfast, lunch, dinner, charcuterie and tapas. The front area is reminiscent of a Parisian bistro, while the white table linen and hat racks at the back have a touch of the 1930s. ⓐ Biblioteksgatan 5 ⓣ 08 611 4222 ⓦ www.zinkgrill.se ⓛ 08.30–10.30, 11.30–01.00 Mon–Fri, 13.00–01.00 Sat, 12.00–23.00 Sun ⓝ T-bana: Östermalmstorg

Café Opera £££ ⑰ Of the dining/social venues in the opera house, Café Opera is the most exclusive, with superb service and a Continental clientele. Dress well, and hope for the best; the party begins around 23.00, as does the admission charge. ⓐ Royal Opera, Kungsträdgården ⓣ 08 676 5800 ⓦ www.cafeopera.se ⓛ 22.00–03.00 Wed–Sun ⓝ T-bana: Kungsträdgården

Fredsgatan 12 £££ ⑱ Flawless style, with the sober interior and dishes that resemble pieces of art complementing each other perfectly. Housed in the Royal Swedish Academy of Arts, this restaurant lives up to its reputation as one of the country's finest establishments, with an award-winning chef running the kitchen. ⓐ Fredsgatan 12 ⓣ 08 248 052 ⓦ www.fredsgatan12.com ⓛ 11.30–14.00 Mon–Fri, 17.00–01.00 Mon–Sat ⓝ T-bana: T-Centralen

Hälsingborg £££ ⑲ A much-hyped restaurant featuring three themed menus: Farm, Ocean and Forest. Hälsingborg is a small city in southern Sweden and the restaurant's aim is to show the capital what the countryside has to offer. The Champagne Courtesy Bar has champagne tasting with the guidance of a sommelier. Book well ahead. ⓐ Mäster Samuelsgatan 60 ⓣ 08 673 3420 ⓦ www.halsingborg.nu ⓛ 11.30–14.30, 17.00–01.00 Mon–Fri, 17.00–01.00 Sat ⓝ T-bana: T-Centralen

BARS & CLUBS

Absolut Ice Bar Talk about cool, this place is ice-cold. The hefty price includes the silver cape with faux-fur hood, thick gloves and mukluks. Drinks are served in chunky crystal glasses – ice crystal that is, frozen from pure arctic water from Lapland. So are the walls, the bar and even the art. Try the Ice Bear, with blueberry liqueur, elderflower juice and blue Curaçao with Absolut Vanilla. ❸ Nordic Sea Hotel, Vasaplan 2–4 ❶ 08 505 63124 ❾ www.nordicseahotel.se ❷ 12.45–00.00 Sun–Wed, 12.45–01.00 Thur–Sat ❷ T-bana: T-Centralen

▲ *Absolut Ice Bar is so icy cool that you'll need a hat and gloves*

Berns This palatial 19th-century mansion is one of the city's hottest hangouts, with live music, bars and a classy restaurant. It's the darling of Stockholm's yuppies, who don't blanch at the price tag and appreciate that not just anyone can get in (except on a slow night). Dress well, and you'll dance to anything from techno-house to R&B. ⓐ Berzelii Park 9 ⓣ 08 566 32222 ⓦ www.berns.se ⓛ 11.30–01.00 Sun–Thur, 11.30–03.00 Fri & Sat ⓝ T-bana: Kungsträdgården

Fasching The city's best club for jazz, popular with a mixed crowd that makes it refreshingly interesting. The range is all-encompassing, with Dixieland, modern, Afro, Latin and Cool. ⓐ Kungsgatan 63 ⓣ 08 534 82960 ⓦ www.fasching.se ⓛ 18.00–00.00 Sun–Thur, 19.00–04.00 Fri & Sat ⓝ T-bana: T-Centralen

Knast Tucked away in a graffiti-covered basement, this alternative bar attracts the alternative. Great cocktails, fun evenings and a nice backyard have earned the place several nominations since it opened in 2008. ⓐ Upplandsgatan 7 ⓣ 08 411 3311 ⓛ 17.00–01.00 Mon–Sat ⓝ T-bana: T-Centralen, Hötorget

Lydmar An innovative hotel bar with exhibitions and live performances which is decorated like a living room, making you feel right at home. ⓐ Södra Blasieholmshamnen 2 ⓣ 08 223 160 ⓦ www.lydmar.com ⓛ 07.00–01.00 ⓝ T-bana: Kungsträdgården, Östermalmstorg

Nalen Like all Stockholm dance spots, Nalen has a restaurant and bar alongside its two stages. Shows and events cover anything from Swedish comedy to punk, frequently big-name. Some are free, some very pricey. Advance tickets are available online. ⓐ Regerings-gatan 74

❶ 08 505 29200 ❿ www.nalen.se ❸ Check website for event times
❽ T-bana: Hötorget

ENTERTAINMENT

Bio Sture

Cult movies, new and often independent features, and film festivals.
Thankfully, there's no dubbing in Swedish cinemas, only subtitles.
❹ Birger Jarlsgatan 41 ❶ 08 678 8548 ❿ www.biosture.se
❽ T-bana: Östermalmstorg

Kungliga Operan (Royal Opera House)

Past the expansive gold-plated lobby is a splendid opera theatre.
Generous government support makes this one of the most affordable
places in Europe to hear and see grand opera performed, by the resident
ensemble and touring divas. This is also the home of the Royal Ballet;
some days see two different performances. ❹ Gustav Adolfs Torg
❶ 08 791 4400 ❿ www.operan.se ❽ T-bana: Kungsträdgården

Stockholms Konserthus (Stockholm Concert Hall)

Classical and symphonic music, often hosting international
performers, in an art deco concert hall. ❹ Hötorget 8
❶ 08 786 0200 ❿ www.konserthuset.se ❽ T-bana: Hötorget

Stockholms Stadsteater (Stockholm City Theatre)

One of Stockholm's two major stages, the other one being the Royal
Dramatic Theatre. Swedish language performances and 'Soup Theatre,'
with a changing menu of performance and soups daily. ❹ Kulturhuset,
Sergels Torg ❶ 08 506 20200 ❿ www.stadsteatern.stockholm.se
❽ T-bana: T-Centralen

Östermalm & Djurgården

The smartest streets for shopping and nightlife share this eastern side of the city with Stockholm's eco-valhalla, the leafy island of Djurgården. This green paradise with its scrollwork of winding lanes is the perfect antidote to Östermalm's obsession with the chic and trendy. Walk or bike through its gardens, enjoy the water-framed views of the city and explore its museums at leisure. Some of the city's most outstanding attractions are located on Djurgården, so allow plenty of time to enjoy them.

The line between Östermalm and Norrmalm is a blurry one, but for practical purposes Östermalm begins with the very chic shopping boulevard of Birger Jarlsgatan. Anchoring the neighbourhood's southern end is the stunning row of *belle époque* buildings along Strandvägen – where the well-heeled shopper can invest in modern design classics at **Svensk Tenn** (Ⓦ www.svenskttenn.se). Facing onto Nybroplan, where these two streets meet, Stockholm's showiest bit of architecture, the Royal Dramatic Theatre, sets the tone for the streets that lie beyond it. Welcome to Stockholm at its most rarified.

SIGHTS & ATTRACTIONS

Birger Jarlsgatan

Art nouveau and other elegant styles of the preceding decades decorate the façades of this smart shopping street and the smaller streets leading from it. The fanciful architectural embellishments compete with the contents of the shop windows for ostentatious displays rare in this land of Nordic reserve. *Jugendstil* takes a Venetian twist just round the corner of Smålandsgatan, at number 7.

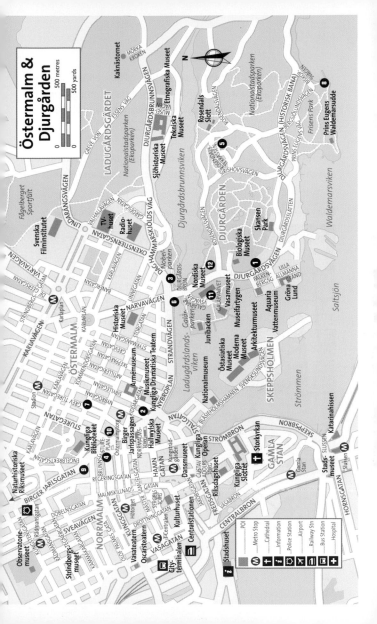

Östermalm & Djurgården

0 500 metres
0 500 yards

Key
- POI
- Metro Stop
- Cathedral
- Information
- Police Station
- Airport
- Railway Stn
- Bus Station
- Hospital

Östermalm
Naturhistoriska Riksmuseet
Observatorie-museet
Strindbergs-museet
Svenska Filminstitutet
Historiska Museet
Armémuseum
Musikmuseet
Kungliga Dramatiska Teatern
Hallwylska Museet
Kungliga Biblioteket
TV-huset
Radio-huset
Kaknästornet

Norrmalm
Naturhistoriska Riksmuseet
Strindbergsmuseet
Kulturhuset
Oscarsteatern
Vasateatern
Dansmuseet
Kungliga Operan
Stadshuset
Centralstationen
City-terminalen

Djurgården
Nordiska Museet
Junibacken
Vasamuseet
Museifartygen
Aquaria Vattenmuseum
Gröna Lund
Skansen Park
Biologiska Museet
Östasiatiska Museet
Moderna Museet
Arkitekturmuseet
Nationalmuseum
Tekniska Museet
Sjöhistoriska Museet
Etnografiska Museet
Rosendals Slott
Prins Eugens Waldemarsudde
Nationalstadsparken (Ekoparken)

Gamla Stan
Storkyrkan
Kungliga Slottet
Kungliga Operan
Riksdagshuset
Stads-museet
Katarinahissen

Bodies of water / areas:
Ladugårdsgärdet
Nationalstadsparken (Ekoparken)
Fågelberget Sportfält
Djurgårdsbrunnsviken
Waldemarsviken
Ladugårdslands-viken
Saltsjön
Strömmen

DJURGÅRDSVÄGEN (HISTORISK BANA)

Just beyond, look into the restored turn-of-the-century shopping arcade, Birger Jarlspassagen. This posh avenue leads straight into the nerve centre of Stockholm's fashionistas and party people, Stureplan.

Gröna Lund

Stockholm's scaled-down version of Tivoli, but just as sparkling clean and charming as its Danish big sister. The roller coaster offers a

It's worth visiting this theatre even if you aren't going to see a show

split-second view of the city that is breathtaking – literally – just before you drop suddenly earthward. Most of the carousels, big wheels and kids' rides are vintage pieces, kept in perfect repair since the park's opening over a century ago. Concerts are held here on summer evenings and cafés dot the pretty park. ➌ Lilla Allmänna Gränd 9, Djurgården ✆ 08 587 50100 Ⓦ www.gronalund.se ⏰ Times vary, May–Sept ⊘ Bus: 44, 47; boat from Nybroplan or Slussen. Admission charge

Junibacken

Astrid Lindgren's lovable character Pippi Longstocking is the star of this kid-centred attraction, where visitors ride a train over rooftops, through houses and across the land of her adventures to do battle with a dragon. Ask for the narration in English, although the sights and sounds are fun in any language. Allow time for kids to explore Pippi's wacky house and dress up in storybook costumes, as well as play the interactive games and watch special events such as puppet shows. Characters from other children's classics may visit, and the excellent bookstore is a good place to find gifts. ⓐ Galärvarvsvägen, Djurgården ⓣ 08 587 23000 ⓦ www.junibacken.se ⓛ 10.00–17.00 Tues–Sun, Sept–May; 10.00–17.00 June & Aug; 09.00–18.00, July ⓝ Bus: 44, 47; tram: 7; boat from Nybroplan or Slussen. Admission charge

Kaknästornet (Kaknäs Television Tower)

Reputed to be the tallest structure in Scandinavia, this communications tower is certainly the ugliest, looking as though it was built by a toddler from sand-coloured Lego. The upside is that from its 152 m (500 ft) elevation you can see the whole city and as far as the archipelago, in a sweeping panorama of islands and water. Restaurant Kaknästornet is at the top, for coffee or lunch. ⓐ Mörka Kroken 28–30 ⓣ 08 667 2105 ⓦ http://kaknastornet.se ⓛ Opening times vary, check website ⓝ Bus: 69. Admission charge (free with restaurant reservations)

CULTURE

The island of Djurgården has the city's highest concentration of museums, anchored by Skansen Park. This historic assembly preserves homes and buildings from all over the country, making it a journey not only into the past, but into the heart of Sweden itself. Another

cluster of museums stands somewhat isolated near the Kaknäs
Television Tower, along Djurgårdsbrunnsvägen.

Aquaria Vattenmuseum (Water Museum)

This world of water and the creatures that live in it fascinates children,
but it's just as interesting for the rest of us to follow the path of a river
from a mountain stream to the sea. Tanks and displays at each stage
show what lives there – salmon, tadpoles, bright coral reef fish, even
sharks. ❸ Falkenbergsgatan 2 ❶ 08 660 9089 ❷ www.aquaria.se
❸ 10.00–18.00 Tues–Sun ❷ Bus: 44, 47. Admission charge

Armémuseum (Army Museum)

It's something of a Stockholm secret that famously neutral Sweden
has such a great army museum. From ruthless Vikings and Stormaktstid
(the Great Swedish Empire, in the 1600s and 1700s) to today's peace-
keeping troops, this is one of Stockholm's most fascinating museums.
Don't miss the Trophy Chamber. ❸ Riddargatan 13 ❶ 08 519 56300
❷ www.armemuseum.se ❸ 11.00–20.00 Tues, 11.00–17.00 Wed–Sun
❷ T-bana: Östermalmstorg. Admission charge

Kungliga Dramatiska Teatern (Royal Dramatic Theatre)

Over-the-top art nouveau in this theatre, built at the height of
Scandinavia's fascination for the style, between 1902 and 1908. One
of the city's most striking buildings, the theatre is where Greta Garbo,
Ingrid Bergman, Lena Olin and Pernilla August all learned their art.
Inside is a virtual museum of art nouveau, from the marble-faced
foyer with its huge ceiling painted by Carl Larsson, to the round,
multi-tiered performance hall itself. Tours (call ahead for times)
explore the backstage as well as the public areas. ❸ Nybrogatan 2
❶ 08 665 6100 ❷ www.dramaten.se ❷ T-bana: Östermalmstorg

Museifartygen (Museum Ships)

Docked behind the Vasa Museum are two historic museum ships (which can be viewed from the dock for free). The *Icebreaker Sankt Erik*, Sweden's first sea-going icebreaker, was built in 1915 and the *Lightship Finngrundet* was one of the country's last operating lightships.

ⓐ Galärvarvspiren ⓣ 08 519 54890 ⓦ www.vasamuseet.se
ⓛ 11.00–18.00 summer ⓝ Bus: 44, 47, 69; tram: 7

Musikmuseet (Music Museum)

Musical instruments – about 6,000 of them from all over the world – are the heart of this museum, but its soul is in the sounds they make. Play with sound in interactive exhibits in the sound room, while kids create their own noise in the Klåjnk, a musical workshop.

ⓐ Sibyllegatan 2 ⓣ 08 519 554 90 ⓦ http://stockholm.music.museum
ⓛ 10.00–17.00 Tues–Sun ⓝ T-bana: Östermalmstorg

Naturhistoriska Riksmuseet (Natural History Museum)

Out of town to the north, this is among the world's largest natural history museums. Exhibits on the prehistoric world and space exploration are especially fun to tour. Ask for an English language brochure, to interpret the Swedish signs and labels. Hands-on exhibits explore outer space and the inner body. Cosmonova, an IMAX cinema, doubles as a state-of-the-art planetarium. ⓐ Frescativägen 40
ⓣ 08 519 540 00 ⓦ www.nrm.se ⓛ 10.00–19.00 Tues, Wed, Fri, 10.00–20.00 Thur, 11.00–19.00 Sat & Sun ⓝ T-bana: Frescati. Admission charge

Nordiska Museet (The Nordic Museum)

You can hardly miss this fairytale castle, with its towers rising above the trees of Djurgården. Swedish culture – everything from its native

Sami population and traditional folk arts and costume to table settings and textiles – is presented in attractive interpretive displays. Portable CD commentaries on the collections are available in English. This is a fascinating place, essential to a visitor's understanding of Swedish culture. The collections (which include well over a million pieces) are overwhelming in scope, so the best plan is to skim most, zeroing in on those of particular personal interest. The shop is well worth a stop, too. ⓐ Djurgårdsvägen 6–16 ⓣ 08 519 54600 ⓛ 10.00–16.00 Mon–Fri, until 20.00 Wed, 11.00–17.00 Sat & Sun ⓦ www.nordiskamuseet.se ⓝ Bus: 44, 47; tram: 7; boat from Nybroplan or Slussen

Prins Eugens Waldemarsudde

Prince Eugen was King Gustav V's brother, and a talented, prolific artist. His home, a three-storey mansion set facing the water, is a landmark on the Djurgården shore. Designed by the same architect as the art nouveau NK department store, the mansion is set in gardens adorned with sculptures by Rodin, and Sweden's own Carl Milles, a contemporary of the prince. Paths lead past a gallery to a large windmill, also overlooking the water. ⓐ Prins Eugens väg 6 ⓣ 08 545 83700 ⓦ www.waldemarsudde.se ⓛ 11.00–17.00 Tues–Sun, until 20.00 Thur ⓝ Bus: 47

Sjöhistoriska Museet (National Maritime Museum)

Indulge your urge to run away to sea here amid models and actual ship interiors. The star of the show is the original cabin and sterncastle of the schooner Amphion, where Gustav III directed his attack on Russia during the 1788–1790 war. Models range from clipper ships to submarines and modern cargo vessels, and throughout the exhibits are navigational instruments, maritime weapons, figureheads,

● *The 17th-century Vasa Ship has undergone an amazing restoration*

seamanship tools and maritime art. A special section designed for children recreates an archipelago land and seascape of boats and boat sheds where they can play. ● Djurgårdsbrunnsvägen 24 ● 08 519 54900 ● www.sjohistoriska.se ● 10.00–17.00 ● Bus: 69. Admission charge

Skansen Park

The concept of open-air museums that gathered together endangered buildings and cultural icons so that later generations could appreciate their roots may have begun on Djurgården. Opening in 1891, this museum of Swedish folk life and culture is a window into Sweden's past, with more than 150 buildings dating before 1900. The oldest is from the 1400s, and the buildings are arranged geographically according

to their origins. Craftspeople demonstrate glassblowing, metal working, weaving and other traditional skills, and you can buy the results in the studios or at the excellent gift shop.

Traditional herbs used for medicines and flavouring grow in the Rose Garden, and a small zoo contains examples of Sweden's native animals, such as reindeer, wolves, brown bears and moose. Spread over 75 acres, the sheer size of Skansen Park means that you could spend most of the day here. ⓐ Djurgårdsslätten 49–51 ⓣ 08 442 8000 ⓦ www.skansen.se ⓛ Daily; opening hours vary ⓝ Bus: 44, 47; tram: 7; boat from Nybroplan or Slussen. Admission charge

Tekniska Museet (Museum of Technology)

Techies take heart! While the art mavens gaze enraptured at paintings, you can revel in what makes the real world tick. Play with the exhibits, do your own scientific experiments, converse with robots or just look at the examples of everything from an 1890s hang glider and World War I fighter planes to classic Volvos and Saabs. The collection is vast, with an entire terrace devoted to flight, from balloons to jet engines. ⓐ Museivägen 7 ⓕ 08 450 5600 ⓦ www.tekniskamuseet.se ⓛ 10.00–17.00 Mon, Tues, Thur & Fri, 10.00–20.00 Wed, 11.00–17.00 Sat & Sun ⓝ Bus: 69. Admission charge (free 17.00–20.00 Wed)

Vasamuseet (Vasa Ship Museum)

On her maiden voyage, the Royal Warship *Vasa* sailed less than a mile before sinking in Stockholm's harbour. The year was 1628, and she lay there in the mud until 1961, when she was raised to the surface and the remarkable story of her restoration began. Be prepared for a shock as you step into the darkened building and see this ship, resplendent in restoration, looming above. You can inspect the Vasa Ship at several levels, peering into the gunports (these were open when the ship began to list, allowing water to rush in and tip the vessel further) and entering the 17th-century seafaring world through displays of shipbuilding, shipboard life and period culture. Begin with the film explaining the history and the salvage process. ⓐ Galärvarvet, Djurgården ⓕ 08 519 54800 ⓦ www.vasamuseet.se ⓛ 10.00–17.00 (until 20.00 Wed) Sept–May; 08.30–18.00 June–Aug ⓝ Bus: 44, 47, 69; tram: 7; boat from Nybroplan or Slussen. Admission charge

RETAIL THERAPY

Some of the city's hottest shopping streets are in Östermalm: Stureplan, Strandvägen and Birger Jarlsgatan. Fashion freaks will find nirvana here, at smart and trendy boutiques and designer shops. Names to look for in stylish yet casual clothes are Anna Holtblad, Filippa K, Gant (actually a Swedish brand; not American, as many believe) and

J. Lindeberg. On the far edge seek out new names including Carin Rodebjer and Carin Wester. If international big brands are more your thing, look no further than Birger Jarlsgatan, where you'll find Gucci, Versace, Louis Vuitton, Mulberry and Hugo Boss stores. Or brave the better-than-thou sales clerks at ABCD for Dior, Fendi and Ferragamo. Just don't look for bargains in this part of town.

Acne If you're into monochrome, slick and minimalistic, this internationally successful Swedish fashion brand is for you. ⓐ Norrmalmstorg 2 ⓣ 08 611 6411 ⓦ www.acnestudios.com ⓛ 10.00–19.00 Mon–Fri, 10.00–17.00 Sat, 12.00–17.00 Sun ⓝ T-bana: Östermalmstorg

Asplund Swedish designers are given pride of place in this showroom, where you'll find furniture, lighting fixtures, rugs and other embellishments for your own space. Look downstairs for bargains on last season's designs. ⓐ Sibyllegatan 31 ⓣ 08 662 5284 ⓦ www.asplund.org ⓛ 11.00–18.00 Mon–Fri, 11.00–16.00 Sat ⓝ T-bana: Östermalmstorg

Birger Jarlspassagen Beautifully detailed wood panelling and a frosted glass ceiling frame the passageway lined with fine shops. Step inside for a sense of what shopping felt like a century ago, but be prepared for 21st-century finds inside, including Agent Provocateur, internationally renowned jewellery designer Efva Attling and the store Mrs H, with brands such as Alexander McQueen and Chloé. ⓐ Birger Jarlsgatan 9 ⓦ www.birgerjarlspassagen.se ⓛ 07.00–22.00 Mon–Fri, 10.00–20.00 Sat & Sun ⓝ T-bana: Östermalmstorg

Modernity If it's art deco, modernism or the classics of Nordic design you seek, seek no further. This Scottish-owned shop has collected

the best examples of 20th-century furniture, art, ceramics and glassware. So if you want to take home a rare piece by Alvar Aalto, Arne Jacobsen or Poul Henningsen, stop here. ➊ Sibyllegatan 6 ➊ 08 208 025 ⓦ www.modernity.se ⏰ 12.00–18.00 Mon–Fri, 11.00–15.00 Sat Ⓝ T-bana: Östermalmstorg

Nordiska Galleriet The Nordic Gallery has managed to stay at the forefront of cutting-edge interior design since the 1930s. Up-and-coming Swedes as well as Eames, Panton, Starck, and the rest of the greats. ➊ Nybrogatan 11 ➊ 08 442 8360 ⓦ www.nordiskagalleriet.se ⏰ 10.00–18.00 Mon–Fri, 10.00–17.00 Sat, 12.00–16.00 Sun Ⓝ T-bana: Östermalmstorg

Oscar & Clothilde This concept store is built around the imaginary tale of English writer Oscar and French intellectual Clothilde, corresponding while travelling the world (read their letters on the website), and starting a boutique with the 'gatherings and scatterings' of their globetrotting days. Delicate 19th-century china, stuffed animals, a Napoleon bust, scented designer candles... The result is a deliciously decadent interior style. ➊ Styrmansgatan 10 ➊ 08 611 5300 ⓦ www.oscarclothilde.com ⏰ 11.00–18.00 Tues–Fri, 12.00–15.00 Sat Ⓝ T-bana: Östermalmstorg

Östermalmshallen Caviar to pheasant, you'll find it in this beautiful food hall. Even if you're not hungry, stop in to feast your eyes on the baskets of orange chanterelles and deep red lingonberries. Lunch is available in any of the several cafés that open onto this lovely food-filled marketplace. ➊ Östermalmstorg ⓦ www.ostermalmshallen.se

---

◀ *As the T-bana doesn't run to Djurgården, there are other ways to reach it*

🕐 09.30–18.00 Mon–Thur, 09.30–18.30 Fri, 09.30–16.00 Sat
Ⓝ T-bana: Östermalmstorg

Skansenbutiken For fine, but not overpriced Swedish crafts, you won't do better than at the museum shop at the entrance to Skansen Park (it's outside the gates, so there's no admission charge to shop there). Finely crafted woodenware in traditional and modern designs, knitwear, furry trolls, painted red Dalecarlia horses, dolls, handwoven table linens, glassware, classic and classy interior decorations, jewellery, pottery and more are shown here. Inside Skansen Park, you can order custom mugs with your name or initials at the **potter's shop** (🕿 08 667 4023) or buy handblown glass at **Glasbruket** (🕿 08 662 8448).

In December, the park hosts a huge Christmas market, where you can find crafts of every type, as well as Swedish Christmas decorations in straw, wood, glass and gingerbread. ⓐ Skansen, Djurgårdsslätten 49–51 🕿 08 442 8268 Ⓦ www.skansen.se Ⓝ Bus: 44, 47; tram: 7; boat from Nybroplan or Slussen

Souk A new haven for younger generation fashion lovers. As Topshop, Topman and Topshop Vintage has taken over the whole upper department floor, smaller women's brands crowd the ground floor. ⓐ Drottninggatan 53 🕿 08 505 74000 Ⓦ www.souk.se 🕐 10.00–20.00 Mon–Fri, 10.00–18.00 Sat, 11.00–17.00 Sun Ⓝ T-bana: T-Centralen, Hötorget

Sturegallerian A classy mall strictly for the well-heeled, with all the names the proper Östermalm local looks for, including Kenzo, Ordning & Reda and Face Stockholm. Here, too, is the spa-to-be-seen-in, the exclusive Sturebadet, and the always fashionable restaurant Sturehof. ⓐ Stureplan/Grev Turegatan 9 🕿 08 611 4606

ⓦ www.sturegallerian.se ⓛ 10.00–19.00 Mon–Fri, 10.00–18.00 Sat, 12.00–17.00 Sun ⓝ T-bana: Östermalmstorg

Svenskt Tenn The Josef Frank fabrics are the most famous, but anything you find at this haute-taste home furnishings design shop will be stunning, as well as stunningly expensive. It's the city's best address in home décor. ⓐ Strandvägen 5 ⓣ 08 670 1600 ⓦ www.svenskttenn.se ⓛ 10.00–18.00 Mon–Fri, 10.00–16.00 Sat, 12.00–16.00 Sun ⓝ T-bana: Östermalmstorg

Victor & Victoria Not so much cross-dressing as a celebration of the female body, with exclusive lingerie brands flattering most shapes and sizes. ⓐ Grev Turegatan 18 ⓣ 08 667 1400 ⓦ www.victorvictoria.se ⓛ 11.00–18.00 Mon–Fri, 11.00–15.00 Sat ⓝ T-bana: Östermalmstorg

TAKING A BREAK

Chic cafés mark ultra-smart Östermalm, but you can still find a few modest places for lunch or a break from shopping. The museums of Djurgården offer excellent cafés and espresso bars, as well as plenty of places to picnic in good weather. Skansen Park has several choices for lunch or a refreshment stop.

Blå Porten £–££ ❶ Have a coffee in the dazzling garden or enjoy the celebrated lunch buffet. ⓐ Djurgårdsvägen 64 ⓣ 08 663 8759 ⓦ www.blaporten.com ⓛ 11.00–22.00 Mon–Fri, 11.00–19.00 Sat & Sun ⓝ Bus: 44, 47; tram: 7

Dramatenterrassen £–££ ❷ Bask in the summer sun as you tuck into hearty Swedish specialities or sip a tall cool one from a frosted glass.

The terrace is a rite of summer, part of Dramatens Restauranger, adjoining the Royal Dramatic Theatre. ❸ Nybrogatan 6 ❶ 08 665 6143 ⓦ www.rest-terrassen.gastrogate.com ⓛ 11.30–15.00 Mon, 11.30–22.00 Tues–Thur, 11.30– 00.00 Fri & Sat, mid-June–Aug ⓝ T-bana: Östermalmstorg

Fiore ££ ❸ Close to the bridge to Djurgården, Fiore is a stylish place for a good lunch or for a champagne brunch at weekends. ❸ Strandvägen 56 ❶ 08 528 09800 ⓦ www.fiorerestaurant.se ⓛ 12.00–00.00 ⓝ Bus: 69, 44, 47

Pontus! ££ ❹ Famous restaurateur Pontus Frithiof serves healthy lunches in stunningly beautiful premises. ❸ Brunnsgatan 1 ❶ 08 545 27300 ⓦ www.pontusfrithiof.com ⓛ 11.30–14.00, 17.00–00.00 Mon–Wed, 11.30–14.00, 17.00–01.00 Thur, 11.30–14.00, 16.00–02.00 Fri, 17.00–01.00 Sat ⓝ T-bana: Östermalmstorg

Rosendals Trädgård ££ ❺ The buffet lunch at this garden centre is a work of art, a flower-decked table covered with beautiful dishes of organic ingredients (many grown right here). The breads are served fresh from the oven. In the shop you can buy farm-made jams and artisanal cheeses. ❸ Rosendalsterrassen 12, Djurgården ❶ 08 545 81270 ⓦ www.rosendalstradgard.se ⓛ 11.00–17.00 Mon–Fri, 11.00–18.00 Sat & Sun, May–Sept; 11.00–16.00 Tues–Sun, Oct–Sept ⓝ Bus: 47

Strandbryggan ££ ❻ Stop any time for coffee, or for a meal of home-style Western Swedish favourites, at this waterfront poseurs' paradise. ❸ Djurgårdsbron ❶ 08 660 3714 ⓦ www.strandbryggan.se ⓛ 10.00–01.00 May–Sept ⓝ Bus: 44, 47, 69, 76; tram: 7

AFTER DARK

Stockholm's trendiest bars are in the Sturegatan area, the street itself lined with cutting outer-edge bars and cafés where the glitterati hang out. Prices are what you'd expect in places where people go to be seen. Likewise, the restaurant scene is high-end, but it's hard to keep up with the darling of the moment. Be sure to get up-to-the-minute local advice if such things matter to you.

RESTAURANTS

Hotellet ££ ❼ The darling of the neighbourhood yuppies and style clones, Hotellet is still a good place to be and see – and to eat. The mix-match menu in The Grill offers grilled meats and seafood – veal, lamb, tuna, salmon, chicken or steak – sauced to order with green peppercorn, sherried braised onions, classic béarnaise, chilli hollandaise or other choices. The 13.7 m (45 ft) bar is the local catwalk for hip designers. In the summer, stretch out on the back lawn with your drink. ⓐ Linnégatan 18 ❶ 08 442 8900 ⓦ www.hotellet.info ⓛ 17.00–00.00 Mon & Tues, 17.00–01.00 Wed & Thur, 16.00–01.00 Fri, 18.00–01.00 Sat ⓝ T-bana: Östermalmstorg

Lisa på Udden ££ ❽ Like its sister restaurant in Östermalm, Lisa på Udden specialises in fresh fish. Add the waterside setting, the view and the excellent wine list to the moderate prices and it's easy to see why a reservation is a good idea on a summer's evening. ⓐ Biskopsvägen 7 ❶ 08 660 9475 ⓦ www.lisapaudden.se ⓛ 11.30–22.00 Mon–Fri, 12.00–22.00 Sat, 12.00–20.00 Sun ⓝ Bus: 44, 47

Vassa Eggen Steak House ££ ❾ The crowd is young, the food is good (if you like steak), the décor chic and understated. This is a place for those who enjoy a good Dakota Ribeye or Nebraska Beef. ⓐ Birger Jarlsgatan 29 ⓣ 08 216 169 ⓦ www.vassaeggen.com ⓛ 11.30–14.00 & 17.00–23.00 Mon–Fri, 17.00–23.00 Sat ⓝ T-bana: Östermalmstorg

Sturehof ££–£££ ⑩ For all its size and popularity, this brasserie remains cheerful, friendly and good value, with enough separate spaces and styles to make everyone happy. An outdoor café, bar and lounge satisfy various drinking crowds, while others head for the large dining room for excellent seafood, served until 01.00. If you're lucky, lingonberry fudge pie will be on the dessert menu. Obaren is the late-night club, with a DJ and occasional live hip hop, soul and rock. ⓐ Stureplan 2 ⓣ 08 440 5730 ⓦ www.sturehof.com ⓛ 11.00–02.00 Mon–Fri, 12.00–02.00 Sat, 13.00–02.00 Sun ⓝ T-bana: Östermalmstorg

Josefina £££ ⑪ An unabashedly luxurious restaurant made for romantic aperitifs under the oaks of Djurgården. Dine like royalty under sparkling chandeliers in a breathtaking, all-white restaurant with floor-to-ceiling windows facing the sea. For those keen on trying Swedish cuisine, there's an extensive menu of local specialities from which to choose. During the warmer months, DJs spin the latest tunes on the terrace. ⓐ Galärvarvsvägen 10 ⓣ 08 664 1004 ⓦ www.josefina.nu ⓛ 10.00–01.00; times vary according to weather ⓝ Bus: 44, 47, 69, 76; tram: 7; boat from Nybroplan or Slussen

Ulla Winbladh £££ ⑫ This restaurant in an historic building does best with the traditional Swedish classics, such as meatballs or venison with wild mushrooms. You can dine outdoors in the summer. ⓐ Rosendalsvägen 8 ⓣ 08 534 89701 ⓦ www.ullawinbladh.se ⓛ 11.30–22.00 Mon, 11.30–23.00 Tues–Fri, 12.30–23.00 Sat, 12.30–22.00 Sun ⓝ Bus: 44, 47

BARS & CLUBS

Spy Bar Constantly reinventing itself by hiring new generations of DJs and interior designers, Spy Bar is one of the safest bets for a great night out. The grand, once privately owned apartment doesn't get swinging until after midnight. ⓐ Birger Jarlsgatan 20 ⓣ 08 545 07655 ⓦ www.spybar.se ⓛ 22.00–05.00 Wed–Sat ⓝ T-bana: Östermalmstorg ⓘ Minimum age 23. Admission charge

Sturecompagniet Very fashionable, very expensive and very hard to get in: the nightclub's five dance floors are filled with cool people sweating onto the very best designer labels. The décor is a draw, along with the chance (however slim) of spotting somebody important. ⓐ Sturegatan 4 ⓣ 08 545 07670 ⓦ www.sturecompagniet.se ⓛ 22.00–03.00 Thur–Sat ⓝ T-bana: Östermalmstorg

THEATRE & MUSIC

Cirkus Built in 1892 to house the many touring circuses that visited Stockholm, the restored Cirkus lives on as a venue for musical performances, and is the favourite of big-name international acts. The restaurant is open in connection with the performance schedule. ⓐ Djurgårdsslätten 43–45 ⓣ 08 587 98700, box office: 08 660 1020 ⓦ www.cirkus.se ⓝ Bus: 47; tram: 7

Kungliga Dramatiska Teatern (Royal Dramatic Theatre) Swedish film legend Ingmar Bergman directed many of the performances in this art nouveau theatre. Its productions are mostly in Swedish, but when foreign dramatic works are touring, they are staged here. It's worth attending a performance, even if you can't understand it, just to see the smashing interior at its glittering best. ⓐ Nybrogatan 2 ⓣ 08 665 6100 ⓦ www.dramaten.se ⓝ T-bana: Östermalmstorg

Gamla Stan & Södermalm

Despite being neighbours, tiny Gamla Stan and sprawling Södermalm couldn't be further apart. Gamla Stan is all that's left of Stockholm's old town, a warren of narrow winding medieval streets that escaped the wrecking ball of the 1960s tear-it-down craze. Södermalm – or simply Söder, as the locals call it – is brazenly and resolutely new and thrives on the razor-sharp edges of culture, fashion and lifestyle. Tourists crowd Gamla Stan's shop-lined streets, but few stray south of Slussen. These streets remain the province of the young, the hip and the in-the-know. The thing the two neighbourhoods have in common is that each has a higher concentration of gay and gay-friendly cafés, bars and clubs than any other part of the city.

SIGHTS & ATTRACTIONS

Changing of the Guard
The Changing of the Guard ceremony at the Royal Palace (see page 105) takes place to band music daily in summer and three times a week in winter, sometimes with mounted guards. ● 12.15 Mon–Sat, 13.15 Sun, June–Nov; 12.15 Wed & Sat, 13.15 Sun, Dec–May

Evert Taubes Terrass
Beyond Riddarholmskyrkan (Riddarholm Church), a broad terrace overlooks the wide channel of Riddarfjärden, with a great of the City Hall on the opposite shore. The yacht *Mälardrottningen*, now a hotel and restaurant (see page 36), is moored at the end of the terrace.

Fjällgatan
High above the terminal for Viking Ferries, in Södermalm, Fjällgatan

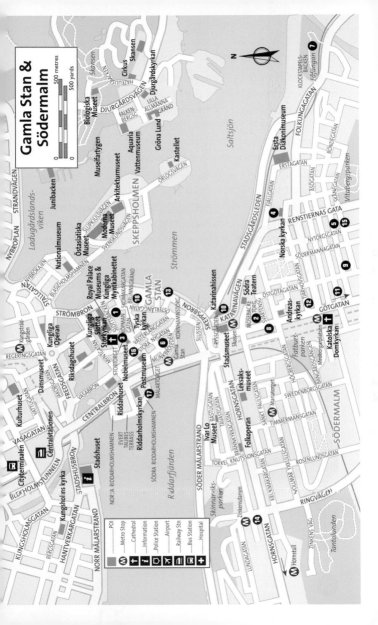

offers expansive views of the entire city. One side of the street is the edge of a precipitous drop, the other a row of historic wooden buildings with very good views from the windows. ⓝ T-bana: Slussen

Gamla Stan

Its buildings dating from as early as the 1200s, a tiny enclave in the heart of Gamla Stan is all that's left of medieval Stockholm. The island's place as the bastion of old tradition is further secured by the Royal Palace crowning its height, where the guard changes and the royal bands march and play in appropriate pomp. These are streets and squares to stroll through, filled with character, lined by shops and galleries and scattered with attractions to visit. Expect to share them with throngs of tourists in the summer, since this is Stockholm's

● *On guard outside the Royal Palace*

most picturesque island. At Köpmantorget you'll meet a determined-looking St George caught in the act of dragon slaying, and around Stortorget, a former market square, you'll see imposing old residences.

Gamla Stan & Södermalm Tours

To see the alleyways of Gamla Stan and explore some corners of Södermalm that you might never find on your own, take a two-hour walking tour of either area. Rich in detail and the little stories that bring these neighbourhoods to life, the tours are led by **Stockholm Stories** (❶ 0708 850 528 ❾ www.stockholmstories.se).

Alternatively, walk through Gamla Stan with an English-speaking guide from **City Sightseeing** (❶ 0812 004 000 ❾ www.citysightseeing.com), visiting hidden courtyards and lanes. Each person in the group (max 20 people) uses individual headphones, so everyone can hear. Tours depart Gustaf Adolfs Torg at 11.30 and 13.30 during July and August.

Katarinahissen

Although, like the other tower across town, it's a bit of an eyesore, the viewing platform more than 30 m (100 ft) above Slussen does give a splendid view over Gamla Stan and the surrounding waters. The fare for the lift is less than a bus fare, or you can impress your friends by bounding up the stairs instead. It's not just for tourists – you'll meet Stockholm families there at weekends; it's particularly nice at sunset. ❸ Slussen ❶ 08 642 4785 ❷ 08.00–22.00 ❷ T-bana: Slussen. Admission charge

Kungliga Slottet (Royal Palace)

Fortresses and castles have perched on the hilltop of Gamla Stan since the tenth century, this one designed in 1697 and completed a half-century later. The Swedish Royal Family lived there until the 1980s, when they decamped to Drottningholm, but their offices are here and you might see them commuting to work any morning. The baroque residence has 600 rooms, and you can see some of them – the ornate reception rooms, the Hall of State with a silver throne, the rococo Bernadotte Apartments, the State Apartments (whose interiors are the oldest in the palace), and Apartments of the Orders of Chivalry. Various other rooms are included in the public tour on a rotating basis, with a different one opened each year. ⓐ Slottsbacken 1 ⓣ 08 402 6130 ⓦ www.royalcourt.se ⓛ Tours in English: 14.00 Tues–Sun, Feb–mid-May & mid-Sept–Dec; 12.00, 14.00, 15.00 mid-May–mid-Sept ⓝ T-bana: Gamla Stan. Admission charge

Riddarholmskyrkan (Riddarholm Church)
The 1270 Greyfriars Monastery is the city's second oldest church, and the royal burial place since medieval times. Its delicate pointed spire is a landmark on the city's distinctive skyline. The three royal chapels include that of the Bernadottes, the present ruling family, whose first king is buried in a gigantic marble tomb. ⓐ Riddarholmen, over Riddarholmsbron bridge ⓣ 08 402 6130 ⓦ www.royalcourt.se ⓛ 10.00–16.00 mid-May–mid-Sept; 10.00–17.00 June–Aug ⓝ T-bana: Gamla Stan. Admission charge

Riddarhuset (House of Nobility)
This beautiful assembly house for the Swedish nobles was built in the late 1600s, at a time when this part of Gamla Stan was filled with such elegant buildings. The gardens surrounding it are perfectly kept, as is the building, which is still the meeting place of the nobility. The meeting hall inside is decorated with more than 2,000 coats of arms of noble families. ⓐ Riddarhustorget 10, off Myntgatan

⚊ 08 723 3990 **Ⓦ** www.riddarhuset.se **🕐** 11.30–12.30 Mon–Fri
Ⓝ T-bana: Gamla Stan. Admission charge

Storkyrkan (Stockholm Cathedral)

The cathedral is Stockholm's oldest church, built as a parish church in the 1200s by Birger Jarl, the city's founder. Its greatest art treasure is the 500-year-old wood sculpture of St George and the Dragon, which experts consider the finest late Gothic artwork in Northern Europe. Although it is believed to contain relics of St George, its real significance to the Swedes is that it represents to them Sweden's defeat of its arch-enemy, Denmark, in 1657. **ⓐ** Trångsund 1 **⚊** 08 723 3016
Ⓦ www.stockholmsdomkyrkoforsamling.se **🕐** 09.00–16.00
Ⓝ T-bana: Gamla Stan

CULTURE

Kungliga Myntkabinettet (King's Coin Cabinet)

Filled with antique coins dating as far back as ancient Greece, the museum (within the Royal Palace Museums) also displays the world's first banknote and the world's largest coin, weighing 250 pounds. Labelling of these and the interactive displays on the history of money is in English and Swedish. **ⓐ** Slottsbacken 6
⚊ 08 519 55304 **Ⓦ** www.myntkabinettet.se **🕐** 10.00–16.00
Ⓝ T-bana: Gamla Stan. Admission charge

Nobelmuseet (Nobel Museum)

If you have a fascination for one of the world's highest honours, the Nobel Prize, or those who have won it, you will find this museum interesting. The theatre shows short films about the laureates – from famous men and women like Marie Curie and Ernest Hemingway to now forgotten but equally important names – and sound booths allow you to hear the moving acceptance speeches. ❸ Stortorget, off Kåkbrinken or Trångsund ❶ 08 534 81800 ❼ www.nobelmuseum.se ❿ 11.00–20.00 Tues, 11.00–17.00 Wed–Sun, Oct–May; 10.00–17.00 Wed–Mon, 10.00–20.00 Tues, June–Sept ❻ T-bana: Gamla Stan. Admission charge

Royal Palace Museums

The Skattkammaren (Treasury) houses the crown jewels – a glittering collection of crowns, orbs and royal regalia that includes King Gustav Vasa's state sword. The Tre Kronor Museum, in the cellars of the Royal Palace, shows the remains of the Tre Kronor castle, built in the 1200s and destroyed by fire in 1697, and relates its history. ❸ Slottsbacken 1 ❶ 08 402 6130 ❼ www.royalcourt.se ❿ 10.00–16.00 15–31 May & 1–14 Sept; 10.00–17.00 June–Aug; 12.00–15.00 Tues–Sun, mid-Sept– Dec & Feb–mid-May ❻ T-bana: Gamla Stan. Admission charge

Stadsmuseet (Stockholm City Museum)

The history of Stockholm and its inhabitants told in pictures, objects and films. This is the largest municipal museum in Sweden and holds some 300,000 items of historical interest, which gives a great perspective on the city's complex history. If you're lucky, you might even stumble upon one of the theatrical events or dance nights organised regularly in the courtyard. ❸ Ryssgården, Slussen ❶ 08 508 31620 ❼ www.stadsmuseet.se ❿ 11.00–17.00 Tues–Sun, 11.00–20.00 Thur ❻ T-bana: Slussen

RETAIL THERAPY

Gamla Stan's streets are filled with tiny shops selling everything from the naff to the nifty. Österlånggatan is the centre for antique shops, especially those with maritime antiques. Västerlånggatan is just as packed, with small art galleries, handcraft studios and co-ops, boutiques and souvenir shops completing the mix there. Tiny alleys radiate from it, with cafés, restaurants and more shops. Södermalm's shopping scene is quite different, of course. Here, young designers have opened label boutiques; retro is in, anything over 35-max is out and alternative is the keyword. Its main drag is Götgatan, one of the trendiest shopping streets in this trendy town, and its shopping arcade Brunogallerian. Giving it a run for its money is a burgeoning area called SoFo – south of Folkungagatan – alive with designer shops.

Blås & Knåda Contemporary designs in glass and ceramics in eclectic styles – and at high prices. ❸ Hornsgatan 26 ☎ 08 642 7767 ⓦ www.blasknada.com 🕒 11.00–18.00 Tues–Fri, 11.00–16.00 Sat, 12.00–16.00 Sun Ⓝ T-bana: Mariatorget

Brunogallerian Near Slussen, this glass-encased mini-mall (the locals just call it Bruno) is packed with Swedish designers' shops, including Filippa K and Whyred. ❸ Götgatan 36 ☎ 08 641 2751 ⓦ www.brunogotgatsbacken.se 🕒 11.00–19.00 Mon–Fri, 11.00–17.00 Sat, 12.00–17.00 Sun Ⓝ T-bana: Slussen

Coctail If you're tired of Swedish minimalism, you'll love this cocktail of all things kitsch, with plastic and pastel the dominant theme. ❸ Skånegatan 71 ☎ 08 642 0740 ⓦ www.coctail.nu 🕒 12.00–18.00 Mon–Fri, 11.00–17.00 Sat, 12.00–16.00 Sun Ⓝ T-bana: Medborgarplatsen

Ekovaruhuset A shop completely dedicated to eco-fashion, with branches in New York and Paris. Well worth a visit for the fashion-conscious as well as the environmentally conscious. ⓐ Österlånggatan 28 ⓣ 08 229 845 ⓦ www.ekovaruhuset.se ⓛ 11.00–18.00 Mon–Fri, 11.00–16.00 Sat & Sun ⓝ T-bana: Gamla Stan

Fifth Avenue Shoe Repair A Swedish designer in the heart of SoFo, a fave with stylistas who crave minimalist and monochrome. ⓐ Bondegatan 46B ⓣ 08 642 8055 ⓦ www.shoerepair.se ⓛ 11.00–18.00 Tues–Fri, 12.00–17.00 Sat ⓝ T-bana: Medborgarplatsen

Gamla Stans Hantverk Beautifully crafted work in paper, wood, leather and other media. Designs range from traditional to modern Swedish, something for every taste. ⓐ Västerlånggatan 27 ⓣ 08 411 0149 ⓛ 10.00–18.00 Mon–Fri, 10.00–16.00 Sat ⓝ T-bana: Gamla Stan

Kalikå If there are any children in your life, do them a favour and pop in here. You'll feel like Alice on mushrooms when you see the fully stocked kitchen and hardware 'departments' with perfectly crafted miniatures of adult tools and utensils. Clever finger puppets represent animals, storybook characters and mythological beasties; costumes promise to transform kids into Vikings or princesses. Prices are surprisingly reasonable for the high quality. There's another branch in Södermalm, on Ringvägen, next to the Clarion Hotel. ⓐ Österlånggatan 18 ⓣ 08 205 219 ⓦ www.kalika.se ⓛ 11.00–18.00 Mon–Fri, 10.00–16.00 Sat, 11.00–15.00 Sun ⓝ T-bana: Gamla Stan

Lisa Larsson Secondhand For yesterday's styles from every era, look no further. You can join the Mod Squad or look as though you've just stepped off the set of a Garbo flick. ⓐ Bondegatan 48 ⓣ 08 643 6153 ⓦ www.lisalarssonsecondhand.com ⓛ 13.00–18.00 Tues–Fri, 11.00–15.00 Sat ⓝ T-bana: Medborgarplatsen

Ljunggrens Pappershandel A wonderland of paper, from delicate, tissue-thin sheets to hefty, handmade card-weight fills neat rows of cubby-hole shelves and hangs from rods like newspapers in a Viennese café. ⓐ Köpmangatan 3 ❶ 08 676 0383 ⓦ www.ljunggrenspapper.com ⓛ 11.00–18.00 Tues–Fri, 11.00–15.00 Sat; closed Sat, July & Aug ⓝ T-bana: Gamla Stan

Nudie Jeans This Swedish jeans brand has a fit for every bottom. The flagship store is a haven for the young and trendy. ⓐ Skånegatan 75 ❶ 08 410 97200 ⓦ www.nudiejeans.com ⓛ 11.00–18.30 Mon–Fri, 11.00–16.30 Sat, 12.00–16.00 Sun ⓝ T-bana: Medborgarplatsen

⬤ *Explore the cobbled streets of Gamla Stan, lined with shops and cafés*

Överdraget Design In the mood for a home make-over? Browse cloth and covers in beautiful Nordic colours and patterns, designed by the owner for anything that demands a fresh new look – sofas, cushions, chairs or beds. **ⓐ** Köpmanbrinken 6, off Österlånggatan **ⓣ** 08 213 721 **ⓛ** 11.00–18.00 Tues–Fri, 11.00–15.00 Sat **ⓝ** T-bana: Gamla Stan

Scaramouche Long to be a medieval minstrel? A Viking maiden? A court jester? Or perhaps a Renaissance king? Indulge your fantasy in authentic historic garb from this step-back-in-time costume shop. Fine replicas of ancient glassware and other historic repros, too. **ⓐ** Kornhamnstorg 47 **ⓣ** 08 102 523 **ⓦ** www.scaramouche.se **ⓛ** 12.00–18.00 Tues–Fri, 11.00–16.00 Sat & Sun **ⓝ** T-bana: Gamla Stan

Sweden Bookshop The undisputed home of books about Sweden. Learn more about art, architecture or history, peruse Swedish classics, and splash out on glossy coffee-table books in your own language. **ⓐ** Slottsbacken 10 **ⓣ** 08 453 7880 **ⓦ** www.swedenbookshop.com **ⓛ** 10.00–18.00 Mon–Fri, 11.00–16.00 Sat **ⓝ** T-bana: Gamla Stan

Tjallamalla For clothes and accessories that are young and not what everyone else is wearing, Tjallamalla is the place. New young designers have a friend here in SoFo, where many of today's established designers started out. **ⓐ** Bondegatan 46 **ⓣ** 08 640 7847 **ⓦ** www.tjallamalla.com **ⓛ** 12.00–18.00 Mon–Fri, 12.00–16.00 Sat **ⓝ** T-bana: Medborgarplatsen

Weekday and Monki Streetwear brand Cheap Monday, ignored for its 'satanic' skull logo in secular Sweden, caused a furore among conservative Christians in the US. Now it's worn by young Hollywood as well as local teenagers. Slip next door to sister chain Monki for

even more cutting-edge fashion. ⓐ Götgatan 21 ① 08 642 1772
ⓦ www.weekday.se ① 11.00–20.00 Mon–Fri, 11.00–18.00 Sat,
12.00–17.00 Sun Ⓝ T-bana: Slussen

TAKING A BREAK

Chokladkoppen £ ❶ Have lunch on the big veranda or in the vaults
of this much appreciated, gay-friendly café in the heart of Gamla Stan.
ⓐ Stortorget 18, off Kåkbrinken, Skomakargatan or Trångsund
① 08 203 170 ① 08.00–23.00 Ⓝ T-bana: Gamla Stan

Fyra Knop £ ❷ A cheap, bohemian 'hole in the wall', crêperie Fyra
Knop has remained untouched in the Götgatan gentrification process.
Try a galette with ham and Roquefort cheese, or a chocolate crêpe if
you're just peckish. ⓐ Svartensgatan 4 ① 08 640 7727 ① 17.00–23.00
Mon–Fri, 12.00–23.00 Sat & Sun Ⓝ T-bana: Slussen, Medborgarplatsen

Grillska Husets Café £ ❸ Enjoy a lunch buffet with freshly baked
bread in an historical building from the 17th century. Some of the
profit goes to the homeless. ⓐ Stortorget 3 ① 08 787 8605
① 10.00–18.00 Mon–Fri Ⓝ T-bana: Gamla Stan

Hermans £ ❹ An all-you-can-eat vegetarian buffet is served daily at
very reasonable prices. You can eat in the garden with a view over the
city, in a gay-friendly environment. ⓐ Fjällgatan 23 ① 08 643 9480
ⓦ www.hermans.se ① 11.00–23.00 Ⓝ Bus: 3, 53, 66

Primo Ciao Ciao £ ❺ The pizzeria offers blankets to warm you
on chilly days at their alfresco café. The grilled veggie pizza with
rocket is scrumptious and prices wallet-friendly. ⓐ Bondegatan 44

📞 08 640 0110 🕐 10.00–21.00 Mon–Fri, 12.00–21.00 Sat & Sun
🚇 T-bana: Medborgarplatsen

Café Tabac £–££ ❻ Sit by the bar in this spicy, Spanish-inspired café and watch people stroll by on the Gamla Stan square as you munch your tapas, or have dinner in the buzzy restaurant out back. 📍 Stora Nygatan 46 📞 08 101 534 🕐 10.00–00.00 Mon–Thur, 10.00–01.00 Fri & Sat, 12.00–00.00 Sun 🚇 T-bana: Gamla Stan

Fåfängans Café £–££ ❼ For a peaceful place to watch the sun set over the city, hop on a bus to Södermalm heights and have coffee at this garden café. 📍 Klockstapelsbacken 3 📞 08 642 9900 🌐 www.fafangan.se 🕐 11.00–13.30 Sat & Sun, Jan–Apr; 11.00–20.00 May; 11.00–22.00 June–Aug; 11.00–16.00 Sept 🚌 Bus: 3, 53, 66

Ljunggren ££ ❽ Join the fashionistas for sushi and sashimi in this stylish enclave inside Brunogallerian. 📍 Götgatan 36 📞 08 640 7565 🌐 www.restaurangljunggren.se 🕐 11.30–16.00 Mon–Fri, 17.00–00.00 Mon & Tue, 17.00–01.00 Wed–Sat 🚇 T-bana: Slussen

Pet Sounds Bar ££ ❾ A well-known record shop that now also encompasses a trendy restaurant with award-winning crossover cuisine. Try to get your table early, as the bar fills up with beer-drinking hipsters an hour or so before midnight. Don't miss the occasional impromptu performance by a visiting star on the downstairs stage. 📍 Skånegatan 80 📞 08 643 8225 🌐 www.petsoundsbar.se 🕐 17.00–00.00 Tues, 17.00–01.00 Wed–Sat, 15.00–00.00 Sun 🚇 T-bana: Medborgarplatsen

Eriks Gondolen ££–£££ ❿ The view from this lofty location above

Slussen is enough reason to head here to unwind after a shopping spree or a tour of the palace, but the skill of their renowned mixologists has reached celebrity status. Owner and chef Erik Lallerstedt is a legend in culinary circles the world over, and has been awarded masses of trophies and medals. ⓐ Stadsgården 6, off Östra Slussgatan ⓘ 08 641 7090 ⓦ www.eriks.se ⓛ 17.30– 01.00 Mon–Sat ⓝ T-bana: Slussen

AFTER DARK

For the hip scene after hours, head south, straight for Södermalm. There's room for everyone, whatever your lifestyle, as long as you have an open mind. Prices run the gamut, without ever approaching those of Östermalm. The hippest is the area called SoFo, with Nytorget at its centre. This is the heart of gay Stockholm, too, with plenty of choices for both gays and lesbians. Gamla Stan is worth a stop for its cosy bars (it, too, has several that are gay faves) and fine dining.

RESTAURANTS

Pelikan £–££ ⓫ Dining places don't get much more classic than this large art nouveau hall with its tiled floor, wood panelling and *Jugendstil* (a northern European take on art nouveau) painted ceiling, not to mention the Swedish comfort-food menu and the schnapps and beer. It was popular long before Södermalm was, and has survived long enough to be appreciated again. Meatballs, of course, are a speciality, and so is herring, but you can also get venison with artichoke or grilled wild duck; daily specials are often bargains. ⓑ Blekingegatan 40 ⓘ 08 556 09092 ⓦ www.pelikan.se ⓛ 16.00–01.00 Mon–Thur, 13.00–01.00 Fri & Sat, 13.00–00.00 Sun ⓝ T-bana: Skanstull

Kvarnens Restauranger ££ ⑫ A funky beer hall where you can get good Swedish home-style meals or something a bit more continental. The bar in the rear, H2O, is a little more intimate than the always-crowded one in front. ❸ Tjärhovsgatan 4 ❶ 08 643 0380 Ⓦ www.kvarnen.com Ⓛ 11.00–03.00 Mon–Fri, 12.00–03.00 Sat, 12.00–03.00 Sun Ⓝ T-bana: Medborgarplatsen

Melanders Skeppsbron ££ ⑬ In an old customs house next to the sea and right on one of Stockholm's most beautiful promenades, the famous fish dealer Melanders Fisk has opened a summer restaurant. Here, the seafood is guaranteed to be of the absolute finest quality. Try specialities such as fried herring with lingonberries, salmon or a classic Toast Skagen, Sweden's seafood version of a club sandwich. ❸ Skeppsbrokajen, Tullhus 2 ❶ 08 225 755 Ⓦ www.melanders.se Ⓛ 11.00–23.00 Mon–Tues, 11.00–01.00 Wed–Sat, 12.00–22.00 Sun, June–Aug Ⓝ T-bana: Gamla Stan

Portofino ££ ⑭ The very model of a true trattoria. Enjoy pure, fresh ingredients and the best carpaccio, vitello, cannelloni and pannacotta in town. Even the service is characterised by a Mediterranean temperament: quick, charming and personal. Be sure to make reservations in advance. ❸ Brännkyrkagatan 93 ❶ 08 720 3550 Ⓦ www.portofino.nu Ⓛ 17.00–00.00 Mon–Sat Ⓝ T-bana: Zinkensdamm

Roxy ££ ⑮ Contemporary Mediterranean-inspired dishes, using fresh local ingredients, make this gay-friendly restaurant popular with a trendy clientele in the local design scene. Begin with a small dish, such as roasted tomato with chèvre cream, or go straight to the mains – perhaps almond-roasted saddle of venison with cep and Manchego

potatoes and pear-chilli salsa. ❸ Nytorget 6, off Skånegatan
❶ 08 640 9655 ❿ www.roxysofo.se ❺ 17.00–01.00 Tues–Thur,
17.00–01.00 Fri & Sat, 17.00–00.00 Sun ❽ T-bana: Skanstull

Tsarskij sad ££ ⓰ 'The Tsar's Garden' is a real Stockholm hotspot,
located in that most romantic of districts: medieval Gamla Stan. This
gold-dipped yet surprisingly affordable Russian delight is perfect for
starry-eyed lovers. Don't spill champagne on your blinis when the
staff let loose the artificial thunderstorm, complete with lights
flashing and the sound of drizzling rain. Pure magic. ❸ Stora
Nygatan 20 ❶ 08 210 404 ❺ 17.00–23.00 Tues–Thur, 17.00–00.00
Fri & Sat ❽ T-bana: Gamla Stan

Mälardrottningen £££ ⓱ A restaurant on a yacht is intriguing,
even for water-bound Stockholm. But the Mälardrottningen takes
this far beyond the novelty value with good food, nice atmosphere
and a superlative sunset view. Start dinner with salmon tartar and
a zucchini timbale, or reindeer salad topped with fish roe, served
in a basket made of crispbread. End with either of the two local
berries – a cloudberry pannacotta with *lakka* (cloudberry) liqueur or
a mousse of lingonberries in a berry coulis. ❸ Riddarholmshamnen
Södra ❶ 08 545 18780 ❿ www.malardrottningen.se ❺ 18.00–23.00
Tues–Sat ❽ T-bana: Gamla Stan

Le Rouge £££ ⓲ Celebrity chef Melker Andersson serves French
and Italian cuisine accompanied by cancan performances under
the vault of Gamla Stan. The theme is Moulin Rouge and the
ambiance unbeatable. Make an evening of it. ❸ Brunnsgränd 2–4
❶ 08 505 24430 ❿ www.lerouge.se ❺ 17.00–01.00 Mon–Sat
❺ T-bana: Gamla Stan

BARS & CLUBS

Mosebacke Etablissement Enjoy the view from the terrace in good weather at this combo bar, café, restaurant, disco and club. Check the schedule, since the music styles vary from jazz to pop to reggae to raw fusion. Saturday jazz brunches also feature live music. ⓐ Mosebacke Torg 3 ⓣ 08 556 09890 ⓦ www.mosebacke.se ⓛ 17.00–01.00 Mon–Thur, 17.00–02.00 Fri, 10.30–02.00 Sat, 10.30–00.00 Sun (kitchen closes 22.00); outdoor café from 11.00 in summer; brunch: 10.30–15.00 Sat ⓝ T-bana: Slussen

Torget The atmosphere of this popular gay bar in the old town seems more like someone's living room. Meals (very good) are served, as well as drinks, to a wide range of music. ⓐ Mälartorget 13 ⓣ 08 205 560 ⓛ 16.00–01.00 ⓝ T-bana: Gamla Stan

MUSIC

Folkoperan Unconventional and avant-garde productions of well-known operas and new operatic works are the speciality of this opera house, whose intimate theatre makes the opera experience even more uncommon. Forget the stodgy image you had of opera – you might like this better. ⓐ Hornsgatan 72 ⓣ 08 616 0750 ⓦ www.folkoperan.se ⓝ T-bana: Mariatorget

Stampen This Gamla Stan pub is Stockholm's first stop for serious jazz lovers, with top live jazz performance. Daily evening jam sessions. All moods of jazz are heard here – Dixie, trad, swing, rockabilly. ⓐ Stora Nygatan 5 ⓣ 08 205 793 ⓦ www.stampen.se ⓝ T-bana: Gamla Stan

○ *A bather leaps off the rocky archipelago shoreline*

OUT OF TOWN

trips

The Archipelago

Less than half an hour from the heart of Stockholm is a watery wonderland of 24,000 islands, a scenic playground where city residents spend weekends and holidays. Some are little more than skerries; others lie in clusters that form mini-archipelagos within.

A steady stream of ferries and historic boats connects these, making day trips or longer island-hopping adventures easy. Romantic lodging, camping, fine dining, local crafts, paddle sports, fishing, sailing, walking trails, historic sights, beaches and a variety of natural environments offer enough attractions to occupy several days. From June to mid-August, everything is open on the islands. In spring and autumn many places are still open, but only a few operate all winter, and the boat service is limited then.

The scenery and the laid-back atmosphere of the islands are the greatest attraction, each island with its own character. Some, such as Gustavsberg and Vaxholm, are connected to Stockholm by causeway or bridge. Boats to the others (and to Vaxholm) depart from Strömkajen and Strandvägen, in central Stockholm. At the tourist office in Sweden House you can book excursions that include boat trips and activities, such as sailing or cycling and even meals and lodging, or you can buy an Island Hopper card, good for five days of unlimited travel on Waxholmsbolaget and Cinderella boats throughout the archipelago.

For further information on the area, contact the Archipelago Foundation, **Skärgårdsstiftelsen** (❶ 08 440 5600 ❾ www.skargardsstiftelsen.se).

GETTING THERE

A trip by boat to any of the islands is an enjoyable excursion, filled with changing scenery from the moment you embark. Many visitors simply take these island ferries for a day on the water, enjoying the meals served on board as they watch the islands float past.

Three companies operate ferries to the islands. The Island Hopper pass for SEK420 gives free passage on Waxholmsbolaget and Cinderella boats. Full schedules for each line are shown on their respective websites or you can pick up printed schedules at their landing points. These are handy to carry with you if you are hopping among islands.

Cinderellabåtarna boats leave from Strandvägen for the major islands. ☎ 08 120 04000 Ⓦ www.cinderellabatarna.com

Strömma Kanalbolaget ferries leave from Strandvägen and travel to the major islands and to Gustavsberg. Many of their excursions include lunch and/or dinner served on board. ☎ 08 120 04000 Ⓦ www.strommakanalbolaget.com

Waxholmsbolaget operates throughout the archipelago, with modern, year-round ferries and historic boats. They board from Strömkajen, in front of the Grand Hôtel. ☎ 08 614 6465 Ⓦ www.waxholmsbolaget.se

SIGHTS & ATTRACTIONS

THE ISLANDS
Finnhamn
Finnish ships bound for Stockholm used to stop here, giving the island its name. Like Grinda, Finnhamn was once the summer estate of a wealthy Stockholm man, who built a summer villa

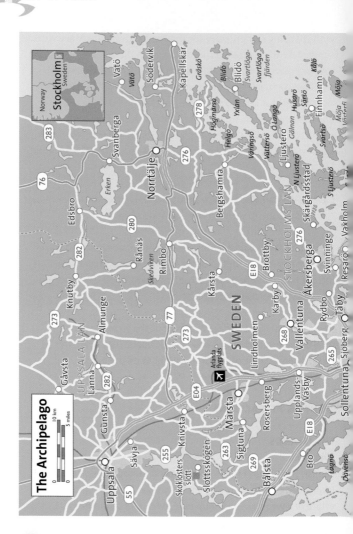

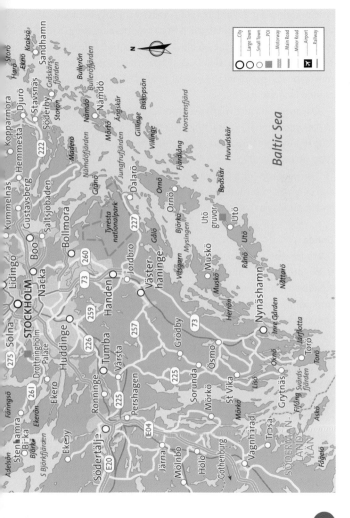

here, and the island was later purchased by the City of Stockholm as a recreation area and to save it from over-development. It, too, is now in the hands of the Archipelago Foundation. The villa has become a **youth hostel** (☎ 08 542 46212), where you can rent rowing boats to explore the several smaller islands that cluster around Finnhamn.

Oak trees and rare wildflower species grow here, among outcrops of flat rocks that are characteristic of these glacially scoured islands. Stop to buy homemade preserves at the farm store at Idholmens Gård, an organic farm.

The boat trip from Stockholm takes about two and a half hours and operates year round. Several boats arrive each day in summer, and at midday a Cinderellabåt stops here on its way to Sandhamn.

Grinda

Owned by the Archipelago Foundation, Grinda is just the right size to explore via the trails that criss-cross its piney hills or by kayak. A paddle around the island reveals the variety of its shoreline scenery, from sandy beaches and coves to rocky cliffs. Kayaks are available at the dock at Grinda Wärdshus. This *Jugendstil* (art nouveau) summer home is now an inn with an excellent restaurant (see page 134). A flock of sheep live on the island's interior, which was once cleared for farming, and they take care of the lawns. Along with Grinda Wärdshus, the island has a hostel, cottages and a camping area for overnight stays. Because the island is a nature and recreation reserve, there is little commercial activity apart from two restaurants and a small food store for campers.

The two jetties, north and south, have year-round boat services to Stockholm, and the island is a good stopover on the way to Finnhamn, reached by a boat from the northern jetty.

⬤ *Spectacular views are enjoyed along with a drink or meal on Grinda*

Gustavsberg

An island east of the city, Gustavsberg lies at the very beginning
of the archipelago, accessible by bus or ferry. The porcelain factories
here date from 1825, but a brickworks was here as early as the 1600s.
The harbour area has recently had a facelift, restoring some of the
fine old buildings to make it a centre for design, crafts, fine glass and
porcelain. The Porcelain Museum, galleries, crafts studios (70 working
artists have studios here), factory outlets, and antiques market,
along with cafés and restaurants are all a few steps from the boat
landing (see page 129).

Within an easy walk are several other interesting sights. The
Round House, designed by the architect Olof Thunström, was built

125

as the municipal building in 1953, and Grindstugatan is the town's oldest street, where you can see artisans' cottages from the 1800s. Farsta Palace is a 16th-century manor house, now private residences.

Tourist Information ⓐ Odelbergs väg 5B ⓘ 08 570 34609
Ⓦ www.varmdo.se/turist 🕐 11.00–16.00 Tues–Sun, Jan–Apr; 10.00–18.00 Tues–Fri, 11.00–16.00 Sat & Sun, May–Sept; 11.00–16.00 Tues–Sun, Oct–Dec

Möja Archipelago

Like Finnhamn, Möja is a whole mini archipelago of its own, and it has even less development. The village of Berg has a restaurant, a little homestead museum, a bakery, a few craftsmen's studios and the Dansbanan, a dance pavilion and social gathering point where they show occasional films. Stora Möja has a few shops and a restaurant and there is a sauna open to the public in Östholmen. Apart from that the islands are the preserve of walkers, cyclists, fishermen and boaters, who enjoy its peaceful natural environments and seascapes. Trails wander through its forests and across its meadows. Bikes and kayaks are available for rent in the summer. The tourist office can arrange lodging in island cottages.

Waxholmsbolaget and Cindarellabåtarna have a scheduled ferry service to Stora Möja from Stockholm daily in the summer; the trip is about three hours. Or you can take a bus from Slussen to Sollenkroka for a shorter ferry ride or to take a **taxi boat** (ⓘ 0708 174 778).

Tourist information ⓐ Berg, Möja ⓘ 08 571 64053
Ⓦ www.mojaturistinfo.se 🕐 11.00–17.00 mid-June–mid-Aug

Nämdö

Another little cluster of islands and islets with Nämdö its largest, this is a place for those who love quiet and nature. Wild deer and elk inhabit the rolling western side of the island and the centre is covered in pine forests. Östanvik, Sand and Solvik are the three ferry stops, and at the first of these is a working organic farm, **Östanviks Gård** (❶ 08 571 56418 Ⓦ www.ostanviksgard.se), and a nature trail. The farm also offers camping and a farm shop.

In Sand, the small **Skärgårdsmuseet** (Archipelago Museum ❶ 08 571 59047 Ⓦ www.skargardsmuseet.org ● 12.00–16.00 mid-June–Aug) shows island handiwork and historic photos. A lookout tower crowns the highest point, Nämdö Böte, at the northeast, which rises to a 40 m (130 ft) elevation. You can hire bikes at Solvik to explore the island. Scheduled summer ferries from Stockholm require a change of boats in Saltsjöbaden, or you can take the bus from Slussen to Stavsnäs for a year-round ferry ride of about one hour.

Tourist Information ❸ Solvik ❶ 08 571 56017

Sandhamn

For the highlife – or at least the archipelago's hottest nightlife – and sandy beaches, follow the yachting set to this island at the outer edge, 48 km (30 miles) east of Stockholm. The Royal Swedish Yacht Club was established here a century ago, with its clubhouse in a 1752 customs house. The main village has been here since the 1600s, although the Russians saw to it that almost none of the original buildings remain. The close-set little red cottages that line the narrow lanes date from the 1800s. For a sense of the shipping that once stopped here, look for the old cemetery at the edge of town, where the stones show names of sailors from all over the world.

Restaurants and shops, tennis and even mini-golf and scuba-diving offer diversion, and trails lead through the piney woodlands to a beach on the opposite side called, curiously, Trouville. THE Trouville it's not, but a lovely beach it is, and less crowded than those nearer town.

The boat trip from Stockholm takes about three hours direct, but it's much more fun to take the boat tour offered by **Strömma Kanalbolaget** (**t** 08 120 04000 **w** www.strommakanalbolaget.com), during which you navigate through the shallow Strömma Canal into the outer archipelago and all the way to Sandhamn. The eight-hour return trip includes a two-hour stop in Sandhamn, with a tour. **Tourist information t** 08 571 53000

Vaxholm

The easiest island to get to, Vaxholm is a one-hour bus ride from central Stockholm, and only a little longer by boat. This makes it the most crowded, of course, so if you hope to stay overnight or eat in a restaurant in the evening, be sure to book ahead. Luckily for those who do choose to stay over, most of the tourists are day-trippers.

It was King Gustav Vasa who first fortified the island in the 16th century, as protection for Stockholm, by building a fortress on a tiny rocky island. It turned the trick, protecting the sea approach to the city from both the Russians and the Danes. As Stockholm's gateway to the archipelago, Vaxholm became a shipping and fishing centre, providing fresh herring to Stockholm by boat. By the beginning of the 20th century, city residents had begun coming here to build summer retreats, eventually 'discovering' the entire archipelago.

The boat or bus arrives into the very centre of town, a broad quay where craftsmen and booksellers set up tables in the summer. The main street, Hamngatan, is lined with shops, cafés and galleries. A short distance and to the left on Rådhusgatan is the town hall and tourist office, facing Torget, a pleasant square where more craftsmen often congregate. Outside town is **Bogesunds Slott** (**a** Bogesundslandet **t** 0734 343 602 **c** Tours: 15.00 Sat & Sun, June–mid-Aug), a castle from the 1600s which you can tour.

Boats leave every 15 minutes (🕐 12.00–16.00 June, 11.00–17.00 July & Aug) for Vaxholm Citadel, whose solid stone hulk guards the harbour. Inside the fortress is a museum (see page 130), a café and a B&B. For excursions in the archipelago, as well as fishing trips, contact **SeaSafari** (ⓐ Kullasundsvägen 39 ❶ 08 541 75700). You can rent canoes and kayaks from **Skärgårdens Kanotcenter** (ⓐ Resarövägen ❶ 08 541 37790).

From Vaxholm you can continue by boat to Grinda or to several other points in the central and northern archipelago. **Tourist information** ⓐ Rådhustorget ❶ 08 541 31480 ⓦ www.vaxholm.se

CULTURE

Several of the islands have interesting little homestead museums that recall life when they were primarily fishing communities. Apart from these, the only museums are in Gustavsberg and Vaxholm.

Gallery Gula Byggningen

Inside the distinctive yellow building facing the harbour is a large exhibition hall that features brilliantly curated changing exhibitions of Swedish design and craft. Along with the Porcelain Museum, it forms the centrepiece of this smart new art and design district. ⓐ Odelbergs väg 9, Gustavsberg ❶ 08 570 13211 🕐 10.00–17.00 Mon–Fri, 11.00–16.00 Sat & Sun ⓥ Bus: 424–440 from Slussen

Gustavsberg Porcelain Museum

The astonishing collection of historic porcelain is beautifully displayed to demonstrate the development of styles and processes. It shows how closely design in fine tableware and decorative china mirrors the

design styles of each era. Particularly interesting is a room showing kitchens of each era to put the tableware in its context. In the studio, you can watch craftsmen create porcelain pieces and hand paint the designs. ❷ Odelbergs väg 5, Gustavsberg ❶ 08 570 35658 ❻ www.porslinsmuseum.varmdo.se ❻ 10.00–18.00 Tues–Fri, 11.00–16.00 Sat & Sun, May–Sept; 11.00–16.00 Tues–Sun, Oct–Apr ❻ Bus: 424–440 from Slussen. Admission charge

Vaxholms Fästnings Museum (Vaxholm Fortress Museum)

Inside the impressive fortress in Vaxholm harbour is a museum showing the history of the citadel and the defence of Stockholm harbour. Scenes of military life are shown, with uniforms and armaments, and other exhibits focus on the archipelago's unique mining history. ❷ Kastellet ❶ 08 541 71890 ❻ www.vaxholmsfastning.se ❻ 12.00–16.00 June; 11.00–17.00 July & Aug; 11.00–17.00 Sat & Sun, early Sept ❻ Boats leave the Vaxholm landing every 15 minutes during museum opening hours. Admission charge

Vaxholms Hembygdsmuseum (Vaxholm Homestead Museum)

The simple necessities of life on an island homestead are explored in this small museum of household furnishings and fishing equipment. Along with a café, the museum has a shop. ❷ Trädgårdsgatan 19 ❶ 08 541 31720 ❻ www.hembygd.se/stockholm/vaxholm ❻ 12.00–16.00 Sat & Sun, June–Aug

RETAIL THERAPY

The former porcelain works at Gustavsberg have become a centre for Swedish design, as well as attracting a clutch of cut-price outlets for brand names in porcelain and glassware. Throughout the islands you'll find small shops and galleries that display traditional island crafts and products. Smoked fish is a good souvenir of these islands.

Antikhuset i Gustavsberg Specialising in historic pieces of Gustavsberg porcelain, the antique shop has a large selection of porcelain animals, figurines, vases and reliefs by Lisa Larson. ❸ Chamottevägen 13, Gustavsberg ❶ 08 570 30577 Ⓦ www.ahg.se Ⓛ 11.00–17.00 Mon–Fri, 11.00–15.00 Sat Ⓝ Bus: 424–440 from Slussen

Galleri Lena Linderholm Bright, vivid and bold designs splash colour all over this cheery shop. It's clear to see the influence of Lena's travels in Provence in her designs for ceramics, textiles and fine-art prints. ❸ Rådhusgatan 19, Vaxholm ❶ 08 541 32173 Ⓦ www.linderholm.se Ⓛ 11.00–18.00 Mon–Fri, 11.00–16.00 Sat, 12.00–16.00 Sun, June–Oct; 11.00–18.00 Wed–Fri, 11.00–16.00 Sat, 12.00–16.00 Sun, Sept–May Ⓝ Bus: 670

Gallery Gula Byggningen In the same building (the original 1825 offices of Gustavsberg Porcelain) as the exhibition hall is a shop featuring works by outstanding contemporary artists and designers. Along with porcelain and ceramics are graphics and works in wool, paper, textiles, glass, wood and metal. Look here for the hottest and newest in cutting-edge design. ❸ Odelbergs väg 9, Gustavsberg ❶ 08 570 13211 Ⓛ 10.00–17.00 Mon–Fri, 11.00–16.00 Sat & Sun Ⓝ Bus: 424–440 from Slussen

Gustavsbergs Konsthall Buy glass and ceramics from some of Sweden's most renowned craftsmen in this little sister of Gustavsberg's art gallery. ❸ Odelbergs väg 9, Gustavsberg ❶ 08 570 13299 Ⓦ www.gustavsbergskonsthall.se Ⓛ 11.00–16.00 Tues–Sun,

Sept–Apr; 10.00–17.00 Mon–Fri, 11.00–16.00 Sat & Sun, May–Aug  Bus: 474

Iittala outlet This factory outlet is a warehouse-like bonanza of porcelain, ceramics, glass, cookware and kitchen accessories. Nearby are outlets for Villeroy & Boch and for glassware by Orrefors and Kosta Boda. ⓐ Tyra Lundgrens väg 23, Gustavsberg ⓣ 08 570 35655 ⓦ www.iittalaoutlet.se ⓛ 10.00–18.00 Mon–Fri, 11.00–16.00 Sat, 11.00–16.00 Sun ⓝ Bus: 424–440 from Slussen

Magasinet i Vaxholm A beautifully refurbished old smithy offers home furnishings with a Swedish touch. ⓐ Fiskaregatan 1 ⓣ 08 541 30505 ⓦ www.magasinetvaxholm.se ⓛ 10.00–18.00 Mon–Fri, 10.00–16.00 Sat, 12.00–16.00 Sun ⓝ Bus: 670

Sommarbutik Handicrafts from the island are sold alongside groceries and locally grown farm products and freshly caught fish, in a one-stop-shop for all things from the islands. ⓐ Finnhamn ⓣ 08 542 46207 ⓛ 09.00–18.00 June–Aug ⓝ Boats: Cinderella or Waxholmsbolaget

TAKING A BREAK

Bistro Framfickan £ Light meals, snacks and good pasta dishes are served here in an idyllic rock-bound cove. Take-away available for boaters and picnickers. ⓐ North Jetty, Grinda ⓣ 08 542 49491 ⓛ 11.00–22.00 early June–mid-Aug; 11.00–18.00 Sat, 11.00–16.00 Sun, May & mid-Aug–early Sept

Café Seglar'n £ A cosy summer café serving hamburgers and sandwiches on home-baked bread. They can also prepare your

picnic basket. **ⓐ** Seglarhotellet, Sandhamn **ⓣ** 08 574 50400
ⓛ 09.00–22.00 Sun–Thur, 09.00–02.00 Fri & Sat

Sandhamnsbageriet £ The famous sailor buns, an island speciality,
are baked here daily. **ⓐ** Sandhamn **ⓣ** 08 571 53015 **ⓛ** 09.00–15.00
Sat & Sun, May–mid-June; 08.00–17.00 mid-June–mid-Aug;
09.00–15.00 Sat & Sun, mid-Aug–late Sept

Strömmingslådan £ Well past Torget, this garden-set café serves
delicious herring, as well as other dishes that are good choices to
take away for picnics. **ⓐ** Fiskaregatan 18, Vaxholm **ⓣ** 08 541 30247
ⓛ 10.00–16.00 Tues–Fri, 10.00–14.00 Sat, Feb–Dec

Magasinet i Vaxholm ££ Enjoy pickled herring on the rooftop
terrace with a splendid view over Vaxholm's fortress and the
boats in the harbour. **ⓐ** Fiskaregatan 1, Vaxholm **ⓣ** 08 541 30505
ⓦ www.restaurangmagasinet.se **ⓛ** 11.00–15.00 Mon–Fri,
11.00–16.00 Sat, 12.00–16.00 Sun **ⓝ** Bus: 670

AFTER DARK

While the islands, except for Sandhamn, are not known for their nightlife,
they are known for a few excellent restaurants. Grinda Wärdshus is
primary among these, with a sophisticated menu based on locally grown
ingredients. Most of the islands' chefs value the locally available
ingredients, especially fresh seafood from the archipelago. Desserts made
with local lingonberries, rhubarb and elderberries are especially good.

Nämdö kök och bar £ A picturesque, à-la-carte restaurant licensed
to serve alcohol. Have lunch, dinner or an ice cream as you look out

over the sea. This place gets very busy in the summer, so do try to book.  Solviks brygga, Nämdö ☎ 08 571 56379 ⓦ www.namdokrog.se ⏰ 11.00–23.00 June–mid-Aug, 11.00–15.00 mid-Aug–June

Wikströms Fisk £–££ A family-run restaurant where owner Rune and his wife Inga-Lill serve the delicacies they catch in the ocean. ⓐ Ramsmora brygga, Möja ☎ 08 571 64170 ⓦ www.wikstromsfisk.se ⏰ 12.00–19.30 June–Aug

Dykarbaren ££ Trendy nightspot and bar in the centre of town. ⓐ Sandhamn ☎ 08 571 53554 ⓦ www.dykarbaren.se ⏰ 11.00–15.00 Wed–Sun, 18.00–22.00 Wed–Sat, May–Sept, 11.00–00.00 mid-June–mid-Aug

Finnhamn Café & Krog ££–£££ The view from the big veranda is splendid, as is the hot smoked salmon for which the restaurant is known. They will pack picnic baskets for you. ⓐ Finnhamn ☎ 08 542 46404 ⏰ 12.00–23.00 June–Aug

Grinda Wärdshus ££–£££ The chef gets seafood from local fishermen and cheeses, fresh berries and vegetables from archipelago farms, and his efforts have twice earned him the well-deserved title of best restaurant in the archipelago. Original dishes share the menu with creative takes on traditional local cuisine. Bookings essential. ⓐ Grinda ☎ 08 542 49491 ⓦ www.grindawardshus.se ⏰ Fri–Sun, Jan–mid-June & mid-Sept–Dec; daily mid-June–mid Aug

Sandhamns Värdshus ££–£££ Traditional old waterfront tavern that's been serving the public since 1672. If you're tired of fish, try the steak with red onions. Booking required at weekends.

@ Sandhamn **☎** 08 571 53051 **ⓦ** www.sandhamns-vardshus.se
🕐 12.00–14.30, 17.00–22.00 Mon–Thur, 12.00–14.30, 17.00–22.30 Fri,
12.00–22.30 Sat, 12.00–21.00 Sun

Waxholms Hotell ££–£££ Fine dining is offered in the upstairs dining
room, while more casual fare is served on the outdoor terrace in summer.
The smoked reindeer is excellent, but if you ask the chef's advice it will
almost always be the fresh fish. Book ahead to be sure of a table.
@ Hamngatan 2, Vaxholm **☎** 08 541 30150 **ⓦ** www.waxholmshotell.se
🕐 12.00–22.30 June–Aug; 12.00–21.00 Sept–May

ACCOMMODATION

Grinda Wärdshus ££ This island retreat is a 45-minute ferry ride from
Stockholm. A county house from 1906-8, it is now a relaxing place to
retreat to for a few days of hiking, bicycling or boating and kayaking
around the island nature reserve. Rooms are comfortable and
attractive. The dining room serves local dishes with international
flair. @ Grinda **☎** 08 542 49491 **ⓦ** www.grindawardshus.se

Hotell Blå Blom ££ Proximity to the harbour, the porcelain museum
and some of Sweden's best outlet shopping; this is a chance to relax in
an inexpensive family-run hotel, easily accessed by bus from Stockholm.
@ Gustavsbergs hamn **☎** 08 574 11260 **ⓦ** http://blablom.se

Waxholms Hotell ££–£££ This pleasant and comfortable hotel
sits right on the quay in a small town at the end of a peninsula.
Accessible by bus from the city, it is still part of the archipelago
and can also be reached by ferry from Stockholm or other islands.
@ Hamngatan 2, Vaxholm **☎** 08 541 30150 **ⓦ** www.waxholmshotell.se

Gothenburg & the Gota Canal

The delightful city of Gothenburg (Göteborg in Swedish) sits on Sweden's western coast, and is filled with attractions little known to foreign tourists. Boat trips on the historic Gota Canal begin from its harbour.

The streets of Gothenburg's old town are a pleasant mix of architectural styles from the 1600s to the present day. A trading centre since Viking times, Gothenburg was home of the East India Company.

Tourist information Göteborg Tourist Office ⓐ Nordstadstorget ⓞ 031 612 500 ⓦ www.goteborg.com ⓛ 10.00–18.00 Mon–Sat, 12.00–17.00 Sun. Göteborg Passes, which give free admission to most museums and attractions, public transport and generous discounts on tours and cruises, are sold here.

SIGHTS & ATTRACTIONS

Liseberg

More than an amusement park, Liseberg is Sweden's most visited attraction, with restaurants, a dance pavilion, live entertainment, music, shops and rides. ⓐ Örgrytevägen 5 ⓞ 031 400 100 ⓦ www.liseberg.se ⓛ Late Apr–mid-Oct, mid-Nov–Christmas Eve ⓝ Tram: 4, 5, 6, 13. Admission charge

Maritima Centrum (Maritime Centre)

The world's largest museum of ships afloat, this remarkable collection includes the only surviving iron-clad monitor, as well as a destroyer, cargo vessel, submarine and light ship. ⓐ Packhusplatsen 12 ⓞ 031 105 950 ⓦ www.goteborgsmaritimacentrum.com ⓛ 10.00–18.00 May–Sept; 10.00–16.00 Fri–Sun, Oct–Apr ⓝ Tram: 5, 10. Admission charge

Masthugget Church

Commanding a hilltop, this striking church uses traditional Viking designs and techniques to create a distinctive Nordic art nouveau style. ⓐ Storbackegatan ❶ 031 731 92 33 Ⓦ www.svenskakyrkan.se/masthugget ❶ 09.00–18.00 June–Aug; 09.00–16.00 Mon–Fri, Sept–May Ⓝ Bus: 85, 87

Trädgårdsföreningen

Gothenburg's Horticultural Society park is a beautiful – and colourful – oasis with a palm house, rosarium and glasshouse, as well as formal beds. ❶ 031 365 5858 Ⓦ www.tradgardsforeningen.se ❶ 07.00–20.00 Mon–Fri, 09.00–20.00 Sat & Sun Ⓝ Tram: 3, 4, 5, 7, 10. Admission charge

CULTURE

Konstmuseum (Art Museum)

Nowhere in Scandinavia is there a finer collection of works by Nordic artists, including Carl Larsson, Anders Zorn and Edvard Munch. An entire gallery is devoted to their genius in capturing the qualities of Nordic light. Prince Eugen is also represented here (see page 89). The Furstenberg Gallery shows early 20th-century Nordic works. ⓐ Götaplatsen, off Avenyn ❶ 031 368 3500 Ⓦ www.konstmuseum.goteborg.se ❶ 11.00–18.00 Tues & Thur, 11.00–21.00 Wed, 11.00–17.00 Fri–Sun Ⓝ Bus: 42, 58, 18, 158; tram: 4, 5, 3, 7, 10. Admission charge

Stadsmuseum (City Museum)

The 1760 East India Building was the headquarters of the company that made Gothenburg a European trade centre for tea, silk, porcelain

and furniture from China and Asia. Now the city's historical museum, it displays Viking relics including the remains of a longboat. ❸ Norra Hamngatan 12 ❶ 031 368 3600 Ⓦ www.stadsmuseum.goteborg.se ⏰ 10.00–17.00 May–Aug; 10.00–17.00 Tues–Sun, Wed until 20.00 Sept–Apr ⓝ 10.00–17.00 Tues & Thur–Sun, 10.00–20.00 Wed. Admission charge

RETAIL THERAPY

In the courtyard around Gothenburg's Kronhuset (Crown House) are craft studios and shops, while the charming Haga district is filled with antiques and speciality shops. And right in the city centre is Scandinavia's biggest shopping mall, Nordstan.

Bebop Antiques with attitude: this shop displays the works of Scandinavian designers from 1900 to the present in a gift-shop setting, not in jumble-sale chaos. ❸ Kaponjärgatan 4 ❶ 031 139 163 Ⓦ www.bebop.se ⏰ 13.00–18.00 Tues–Fri, 12.00–16.00 Sat & Sun ⓝ Bus: 80, 85, 760, 764, 765; tram: 3, 6, 9, 11

Göteborgs Choklad & Karamellfabrik The recipes for fine chocolates and caramels have been passed down through generations. ❸ Kronhusbodarna ❶ 031 775 9064 Ⓦ www.goteborgschoklad.se ⏰ 11.00–17.00 Mon, 11.00–18.00 Tues–Fri, 11.00–16.00 Sat ⓝ Tram: 1, 3, 4, 5, 6, 7, 9, 10, 11

Prickig Katt Designer Malin Leijonberg´s unique hats and jewellery have earned her a reputation throughout Sweden. ❸ Vallgatan 3 ❶ 031 133 350 Ⓦ www.prickigkatt.se ⏰ 11.00–18.00 Mon–Fri, 11.00–16.00 Sat ⓝ Tram: 6, 9, 11

TAKING A BREAK

Most of Gothenburg's museums have cafés, and among the shops of Haga Nygata are cafés with tables along the stone-paved street.

Café Kringlan £ The minute you step into this Haga café with the pretzel sign, you know it's the right place from the aroma of their freshly-baked breads and cakes. ⓐ Haga Nygata 13 ❶ 031 130 908 ❷ 08.00–20.00 Mon–Fri, 09.00–19.00 Sat & Sun ❸ Bus: 80, 85, 760, 764, 765; tram: 3, 6, 9, 11

Markets Saluhallen £–£££ A lively market opposite Trädgårdsföreningen garden, with stalls selling bread, cheese and smoked fish for picnics, and little lunch stands where you can buy a tasty cheap bite. ⓐ Kungstorget 15–18 ❶ 031 711 6791 ❷ 09.00–18.00 Mon–Fri, 09.00–15.00 Sat & Sun ❸ Tram: 3, 6, 9, 11

AFTER DARK

Hamnkrogen ££–£££ You might not expect a restaurant at an amusement park to serve an outstanding meal, but here traditional Swedish dishes mix with trendier fare. ⓐ Liseberg ❶ 031 733 0300 ❹ www.liseberg.se ❷ 13.00–23.00 Fri & Sat, 13.00–22.00 Sun–Thur ❸ Tram: 4, 5, 6, 13

Palace ££–£££ Along with a café terrace on the park, the Palace has a magnificent bar, dining rooms and a nightclub. Dress smartly for this venue preferred by the over-30 crowd. ⓐ Södra Hamngatan 2 ❶ 031 807 550 ❹ www.palace.se ❷ 11.30–23.00 Mon–Wed, 11.30–03.00 Thur & Fri, 12.00–03.00 Sat, 13.00–18.00 Sun ❸ Tram: 1, 3, 4, 5, 6, 7, 9, 10, 11

⬥ *The steps of the Konstmuseum provide a great viewpoint of the city*

THE GOTA CANAL

The Gota Canal, begun in 1607, connects a series of lakes to create a shipping route across the country to Stockholm.

Leaving Gothenburg, the climb through the dramatic Trollhättan locks raises ships more than 30 m (100 ft). Learn about the canal's history at **Trollhätte Canal Museum** (🅰 Åkersbergsvägen, Trollhättan ☎ 0520 472 251 🌐 www.vastsverige.com/trollhattan 🕐 11.00–19.00 June– mid-Aug. Admission charge): start with the informative film (in English) and use the brochure that translates the museum's signs and labels.

At Sjötorp, on the eastern shore of Lake Vänern (Europe's third largest), the Gota Canal proper begins. The last remaining hand-operated lock still in use is at Tatorp, and the oldest house and the oldest lock on the canal are at Forsvik, where a group of singers occasionally serenades passengers with folk songs and hymns.

Across smaller Lake Vättern is an amazing collection of historic and motorised vehicles at the **Motala Motormuseum** (🅰 Hamnen ☎ 0141 588 88 🌐 www.motormuseum.se 🕐 08.00–16.00 Mon–Fri, 11.00–17.00 Sat & Sun, Jan–Apr, Oct–Dec; 10.00–18.00 May, Sept; 10.00–20.00 June–Aug).

As you continue along the canal, across a meadow stands **Vreta Cloister** (☎ 031 60 195), the remains of a 12th-century abbey, Sweden's oldest. The impressive staircase of locks in nearby Berg is one of the most scenic spots on the canal.

Once an important city of the Hanseatic League, Söderköping has preserved its medieval back streets, and the 13th-century brick church of St Laurentii.

Fond £££ Chef/owner Stefan Karlsson is a one-man bandwagon promoting Swedish food culture as a living and dynamic force. He treasures local seasonal ingredients, and the dishes he creates mix Nordic and European traditions with modern culinary ideas and styles. Choose the sampler plate to taste several of the day's different main courses. ⓐ Götaplatsen, off Avenyn ⓣ 031 812 580 ⓦ www.fondrestaurang.com ⓛ 11.30–14.30, 17.00–23.00 Mon–Fri, 17.00–23.00 Sat ⓐ Bus: 40, 45, 58

ACCOMMODATION

Barken Viking £–££ *The Viking* is a four-masted barque, one of only ten remaining, built in 1906. An elegant hotel afloat, it is close to the Opera House. ⓐ Gullbergskajen ⓣ 031 635 800 ⓦ www.liseberg.se

Elite Park Avenue Hotel ££–£££ This newly renovated hotel sits on the city's main street. Rooms are nicely decorated in contemporary modern style. ⓐ Kungsportsavenyn 36–38 ⓣ 031 727 1000 ⓦ www.elite.se

● *Sweden is synonymous with good design, even for the usually mundane*

PRACTICAL
information

Directory

GETTING THERE

By air

As a major European city, Stockholm can be reached by direct daily flights from other major hubs.

From the UK and Europe, **SAS** (W www.scandinavian.net), **Finnair** (W www.finnair.com) and **British Airways** (W www.britishairways.com) all offer as many as six daily flights from Heathrow to Arlanda. **Ryanair** (W www.ryanair.com) flies daily from Stansted to Nyköping Skavsta, often at very low fares.

Most flights from North America require a transfer in another European city before continuing to Sweden. This transfer can be time-consuming since you must go through EU entry formalities, then pass through security points before boarding the second flight. Some companies, including SAS, offer direct flights.

No direct flights are offered from Australia and New Zealand to Stockholm, so the optimal plan is to book the best price to a major European hub with an onward connection.

Although there are fewer ready-made packages to Stockholm than to holiday-in-the-sun resorts, you can sometimes book air fare, lodging and car hire in a budget-friendly package. Ask when booking flights. Especially when booking such a package, it is wise to secure your trip with travel insurance. Most tour operators offer insurance, or you can protect your investment by insuring the trip independently.

Many people are aware that air travel emits CO_2, which contributes to climate change. You may be interested in the possibility of lessening the environmental impact of your flight through the charity **Climate Care** (W www.climatecare.org),

which offsets your CO_2 by funding environmental projects around the world.

By rail

The trip from London's St Pancras International to Stockholm by train takes just over 18 hours, with changes in Brussels, Cologne and Copenhagen, and the trains boarding ferries for the water crossings. Other routes involve transfers from train to ferry for longer crossings.

If you are planning to take lots of long train journeys, it's worth investigating the various multi-day and multi-country train passes offered by **Rail Europe** (Ⓦ www.raileurope.com). For visitors from outside Europe, the Eurail Selectpass permits rail travel in 23 countries, including all four Scandinavian countries (or any combination of them), with even greater savings for two or more people travelling

⬤ *Fleets of ferries link Stockholm with nearby islands, and much further afield*

together. For travellers anywhere, Rail Europe offers a one-stop source of information, reservations and tickets. The monthly *Thomas Cook European Rail Timetable* has up-to-date schedules for European national and international rail services.

Thomas Cook European Rail Timetable (UK) +44 1733 416477; (USA) +1 800 322 3834 www.thomascookpublishing.com

By road

Next to a lucky hit for rock-bottom air fares, the cheapest way to Sweden from the UK is by bus, about 35 hours from London's Victoria Coach Station to Gothenburg or 23 hours to Malmo via **Eurolines** (www.eurolines.com). From Malmo or Gothenburg, continue to Stockholm with **Svenska Buss** (www.svenskabuss.se).

Automobile journeys to Sweden from the UK must include at least one segment by car ferry, which adds significantly to the cost. But this remains a budget-friendly option if several people are travelling together. Sweden, like the rest of the continent, drives on the right-hand side of the road.

By water

Stockholm's location on the Baltic Sea makes boat a popular way to get there from other Scandinavian capitals and northern Europe. Most of these ferries also carry cars, so Sweden can be incorporated into a driving holiday as well.

Denmark, Finland, Norway, Germany, Poland, Estonia and St Petersburg are all connected to Sweden by ferry links, some direct and some through transfers. The two main shipping lines operating these are **Viking Line** (08 452 4000 www.vikingline.se) and **Silja Line** (08 222 140 www.tallinksilja.com).

ENTRY FORMALITIES

Citizens of Ireland, USA, UK, Canada, New Zealand, Australia, Singapore and Israel need only a valid passport to enter Sweden and do not require visas. Citizens of South Africa must have visas to enter. Visa forms can be obtained from the nearest Swedish embassy or consulate.

EU citizens can bring goods for personal use when arriving from another EU country, but must observe the limits on tobacco (800 cigarettes) and spirits (10 litres over 22 per cent alcohol, 20 litres of wine and 110 litres of beer). Limits for non-EU nationals are 200 cigarettes and one litre of spirits, two of wine. For specific questions consult Ⓦ www.tullverket.se. In either case you must be 18 or older to import tobacco products, and at least 20 to bring alcohol.

MONEY

Although Sweden is a member of the EU, it does not use the euro. The local currency is the Swedish krona (SEK), which is broken down into 100 öre. Notes are in denominations of SEK20, 50, 100, 500 and 1,000; coins: SEK1, 5, 10 and 50 öre.

Credit cards are widely accepted all over Sweden, and cashpoints (ATMs) are everywhere. The best means of obtaining local currency is by using a debit card issued by your bank that debits from your own account. Although many banks charge a fee for this, these are usually less than cash advances of credit cards, and are at a more favourable exchange rate than cash transactions or travellers cheques. The latter can be cashed at banks, post offices and in most hotels, as well as larger shops. Currency exchange services are in airports and the central train station.

Banking hours are weekdays from 09.00 or 09.30 to 15.00, Monday through Friday; banks in central Stockholm often stay open until 18.00, and those in airports and other travellers' hubs may be open even longer hours. The bureau de change **X-change** (ⓦ www.x-change.se) at Centralstationen is open every day until 21.00.

HEALTH, SAFETY & CRIME

While you need to be aware of your surroundings in any city, and avoid walking alone at night in doubtful neighbourhoods, Stockholm is not a dangerous city for travellers and has a very low crime rate. That said, petty theft can be a problem anywhere, especially in crowded tourist attractions, so keep money safely out of sight and keep wallets and purses in a secure place. The Centralstationen and Hötorget areas can be very crowded at night, making them a target for pickpockets.

Swedish drivers tend to be very careful, although they do take off from traffic signals at high speed and often travel very close to the kerbs in the city. So be careful before stepping off, even if the pedestrian light shows crossing safe, and stand back from the kerb while waiting at a crossing. Also, take great care crossing bicycle lanes, since cyclists seem to have the right of way over pedestrians in these.

Medical care in Sweden is excellent, with modern clinics and hospitals. Emergency service is available to all visitors. Those from the EU (and a few other countries in Europe) are treated free of charge on production of a European Health Insurance Card (EHIC), which can be obtained from post offices or online at ⓦ www.ehic.org.uk. Those without the card must pay for services, so non-EU residents should carry traveller's health insurance if their own coverage does not include reimbursement, and should also consider emergency medical evacuation insurance, often offered as a package with the former.

OPENING HOURS

Shops generally open around 10.00, staying open until 18.00 or
19.00 from Monday to Friday and closing earlier at around 16.00 on
Saturdays. Museums often close on Mondays. Many restaurants and
smaller attractions operate seasonally, closing for a month or longer
in winter. Banks open at around 09.00 or 09.30 and close at around
15.00, although you will find some banks in central areas that stay
open until 18.00.

TOILETS

Stockholm may have more public conveniences than any other
city in Europe. Every museum and public building has one, and you
can usually use these without paying admission to the museum
(if you must pass an admission desk, just ask for the 'toalett'). Public
toilets are located in all transportation centres and in many other
places throughout the city.

CHILDREN

From high chairs in restaurants and pram ramps on the underground
to a storybook theme park in the middle of the city, Stockholm loves
children. Except in the snootiest of haute-design venues, no-one will
frown at children in restaurants, where the staff will scurry to make
them – and their parents – feel welcome, often with specially priced
children's menus. Most museums have special programmes and
exhibit areas for children, as well as lunch rooms where families
are welcome to eat packed lunches.

Not only does the T-bana have pram ramps and lifts, and buses step-
free entry, but adults with children in prams or pushchairs (strollers)
also ride free on buses; children under 7 ride free all the time on both
buses and the T-bana and those under 12 don't pay at weekends.

Stockholm is filled with places and activities that will keep children amused during your holiday. The island of Djurgården (see page 82) is a particularly fun place to head to for the day, and they'll surely love the boat ride there. Skansen Park (see page 90) is another top kiddie destination, with everything from colourful costumes, demonstrations and folk dancing to a zoo.

At Junibacken (see page 86), children ride a train to meet the characters from the world of Astrid Lindgren's Pippi Longstocking stories, and can play in Pippi's house. At Aquaria Water Museum (see page 87) they'll find fish and other marine life from all over the world, and the amusement park Gröna Lund is just next door. This clean, safe park has rides for all ages and summer concerts that draw performers from all over the world.

Older children will be fascinated by the Vasa Ship and the exhibits in its museum (see page 92) and especially enjoy the chance to stand in a real 'crow's nest' suspended high above the exhibits. At Kulturhuset (see page 66) are libraries, theatres, workshops and play areas for children, most of them free.

For children who like films and electronic games, there's the Museum of Natural History (see page 88) with its IMAX theatre and planetarium, or the Museum of Technology (see page 91), filled with hands-on experiences (including playing with robots).

COMMUNICATIONS
Internet

Internet cafés are common around town and you won't have any problems finding one near your accommodation. Many hotels offer terminals in the lobby for guests, and most have in-room broadband connections for laptops. Almost all of Stockholm is wireless, and many cafés and public areas – such as Kungsträdgården

park – are free WiFi hotspots. A search for 'WiFi Stockholm' on
Ⓦ www.googlemaps.com can also help you locate them.

Phone

The easiest way to make calls in Stockholm is on a mobile phone.
European, New Zealand and Australian mobiles can link to several
GSM networks after changing the band to 900 or 1,800 MHz.
Contact your mobile phone provider for more information. US and
Canadian mobile phones do not work in Sweden unless they are
specially equipped before leaving North America. To save money,
purchase a Swedish SIM card from any electrical store. Note that
making phone calls from hotel rooms is fiendishly expensive.

TELEPHONING SWEDEN

Sweden's international country code is +46, and the code
for Stockholm is 08. To call a Stockholm number from
outside Sweden, dial your own international access number
(011 in the US and Canada, 00 in the UK and Ireland) + 46
+ 8 + local number, dropping the initial 0 before the 8. From
inside Sweden but outside Stockholm, dial 08 and the number.
From inside Stockholm, you do not need to dial 08 before
the local number.

TELEPHONING ABROAD

To make an international call from Sweden, dial 00, then the
relevant country code (UK 44, Ireland 353, US and Canada 1,
Australia 61, New Zealand 64, South Africa 27) followed by the
area code (omitting the first '0' if there is one) and local number.

Post

Post offices take your letters and postcards and are easy to find. You can recognize them by their distinctive logo, a yellow post horn on a blue background.

ELECTRICITY

Current in Sweden is 220 volts AC, 50 hertz. Australian, New Zealand, US, Canadian and some South African and UK appliances will need adapters to fit Swedish wall outlets. If you are travelling in other Scandinavian countries, note that outlets are not all the same. Laptops using only 110 volts will need transformers, as well as plug adapters.

TRAVELLERS WITH DISABILITIES

Stockholm has moved toward accessibility with more enthusiasm than many other cities, a process aided by the Swedish fascination with functional modern design. The underground T-bana system is quite handy for wheelchair users, with lifts and/or ramps (although some of the latter are quite steep) at most stations. Taxis are more difficult than public transport for those who use an electric wheelchair. **SAMTRANS** (☎ 08 522 50000 Mon–Fri) offers transfers to and from airports, train stations and terminals.

Most hotels have fully accessible rooms and some have special facilities so that guests in wheelchairs can use swimming pools and other recreational facilities. **DHR** (☎ 08 685 8000 🌐 www.dhr.se) is a useful information centre for travellers with physical disabilities. Their website is in Swedish but you can get useful information about accessibility in public areas over the phone. There is also a list of accessible restaurants, public toilets and other information on 🌐 www.stockholm.se/idrott (click on "Availability Guide").

The Stockholm archipelago boats operated by **Vaxholmsbolaget** (📞 08 679 5830 🌐 www.waxholmsbolaget.se) are all accessible, with level landings, although the steamboats and several of the other excursion boats are not. At Värmdölandet, in the southeastern section of the archipelago near Gustavsberg, about 30 km (20 miles) from the city centre is Aspvik, a recreation area operated by DHR. They offer rooms and cottages, as well as activities and excursions

TOURIST INFORMATION

Stockholm

Stockholm Tourist Centre (📧 Hamngatan 27, entrance from Kungstradgarden 📞 08 508 28508 🌐 www.stockholmtown.com 🕐 09.00–19.00 Mon–Fri (09.00–18.00 Oct–Mar), 10.00–17.00 Sat, 10.00–16.00 Sun), located at Sverigehuset (Sweden House), offers information on the city and the rest of Sweden, with a well-informed staff ready to answer your questions.

Information about accommodation, as well as a free hotel booking service, is offered by Hotellcentralen (see page 36).

Gothenburg

For information on Gothenburg contact the **Gothenburg Tourist Office** (📧 Nordstadstorget 📞 031 612 500 🌐 www.goteborg.com 🕐 10.00–18.00 Mon–Sat, 12.00–17.00 Sun).

For hotel reservations in Gothenburg, call 📞 031 612 500.

Gota Canal

The main office for the canal boats is in Gothenburg, but you can see the boats when they are either there or in Stockholm, docked in either city centre. For more information on the cruises, call 📞 031 806 315 or see 🌐 www.gotacanal.se.

Emergencies

In any emergency (police, ambulance or fire) dial ☎ 112.

If your car breaks down while driving, contact the Emergency road service on ☎ 020 91 0040.

MEDICAL SERVICES

Should you become ill while travelling, you have several sources of information on English-speaking doctors. The consular office of your embassy can provide a list. You can also go prepared with the appropriate pages from the directory published by the International Association of Medical Assistance for Travellers (IAMAT), a non-profit organisation that provides information on health-related travel issues all over the world, as well as a list of English-speaking doctors (Ⓦ www.iamat.org).

Emergency dentist Ⓐ Kungsgatan 24 ☎ 08 411 1107
Hospital Ⓐ Karolinska Sjukhuset ☎ 08 517 70000

POLICE

Main police station Ⓐ Kungsholmsgatan 43 ☎ 114 14
Police sub-stations Various locations: Ⓐ Centralstationen, Ⓐ Torkel, Ⓐ Knutssonsgatan 20, Ⓐ Brahegatan 49 and Ⓐ Tulegatan 4. Use the main police telephone number above.

Lost property
Central lost property office Ⓐ Klara Östra Kyrkogata 6 ☎ 08 600 1000
Centralstationen lost property office ☎ 08 600 1000

EMBASSIES & CONSULATES

Consulates, and the consular section of an embassy mission handle

EMERGENCY PHRASES

Help! Hjälp! *Yelp!*

Call an ambulance/a doctor/the police!
Ring efter en ambulans/en doktor/polisen!
Ring ehf-tehr ehn ambuhlans/ehn docktor/poleesehn!

Can you help me please?
Kan du hjälpa mig?
Kahn doo yehlpah mey?

emergencies of travelling citizens. Your consulate or embassy should be the first place you turn if a passport is lost, after reporting it to the police. Consulates can also provide lists of English-speaking doctors and dentists and find you an English-speaking lawyer.

Australia Embassy 🅐 Sergels Torg 12 ☎ 08 613 2900
🆆 www.sweden.embassy.gov.au
Canada Embassy 🅐 Tegelbacken 4 ☎ 08 453 3000
🆆 www.canadaemb.se
Republic of Ireland Embassy 🅐 Östermalmsgatan 97 ☎ 08 661 8005
South Africa Embassy 🅐 Fleminggatan 20 ☎ 08 243 950
🆆 www.southafricanemb.se
UK Embassy 🅐 Skarpögatan 6–8 ☎ 08 671 3000
🆆 www.britishembassy.se
US Embassy 🅐 Dag Hammarskjölds väg 31 ☎ 08 783 5300
🆆 www.usemb.se

Editorial/project management: Lisa Plumridge
Copy editor: Monica Guy
Layout/DTP: Alison Rayner

The publishers would like to thank the following individuals and organisations for supplying their copyright photographs for this book: Marie Andersson, page 13; BigStockPhoto.com (Alexander Avdeev, page 21; Sara Holm, page 5; Johan Möllerberg, page 57); Franco Caruzzo, page 67; Centralbadet, page 60; Remus Eserblom/iStockphoto.com, page 40; Everjean, page 35; Olof Holdar, page 63; Åke E:son Lindman, pages 28–9; Log, page 47; Rob & Lisa Meehan, page 7; Mikael Sjöberg, page 17 & 72; Stillman Rogers Photography, pages 19, 25, 44, 79, 84–5, 90–1, 94, 104, 111, 125, 140 & 143; Stockholm Visitors Board, page 145; Henrik Trygg, pages 43 & 119; Vidbynäs Golf Club, page 33.

Send your thoughts to
books@thomascook.com

- **Found a great bar, club, shop or must-see sight that we don't feature?**
- **Like to tip us off about any information that needs a little updating?**
- **Want to tell us what you love about this handy little guidebook and more importantly how we can make it even handier?**

Then here's your chance to tell all! Send us ideas, discoveries and recommendations today and then look out for your valuable input in the next edition of this title.

Email the above address (stating the title) or write to: pocket guides Series Editor, Thomas Cook Publishing, PO Box 227, Coningsby Road, Peterborough PE3 8SB, UK.

WHAT'S IN YOUR GUIDEBOOK?

Independent authors Impartial up-to-date information from our travel experts who meticulously source local knowledge.

Experience Thomas Cook's 165 years in the travel industry and guidebook publishing enriches every word with expertise you can trust.

Travel know-how Thomas Cook has thousands of staff working around the globe, all living and breathing travel.

Editors Travel-publishing professionals, pulling everything together to craft a perfect blend of words, pictures, maps and design.

You, the traveller We deliver a practical, no-nonsense approach to information, geared to how you really use it.

Useful phrases

English	Swedish	Approx pronunciation
BASICS		
Yes	Ja	*Yah*
No	Nej	*Nay*
Please	Tack	*Tahck*
Thank you	Tack	*Tahck*
Hello	Hej	*Hey*
Goodbye	Hej då	*Hey doh*
Excuse me	Ursäkta mig	*Ew-shekta mey*
Sorry	Förlåt	*Feurlot*
That's okay	Det är bra	*Dee air bra*
I don't speak Swedish	Jag talar inte svenska	*Yagh tahlar intae svaen-ska*
Do you speak English?	Talar du engelska?	*Tahlar doo eng-ehl-ska?*
Good morning	Godmorgon	*Goo-moron*
Good evening	Godkväll	*Goo-kvehl*
Good night	Godnatt	*Goo-nert*
My name is ...	Jag heter ...	*Yahg hehtehr ...*
NUMBERS		
One	Ett	*Eht*
Two	Två	*Tvoh*
Three	Tre	*Treh*
Four	Fyra	*Fuhrah*
Five	Fem	*Fehm*
Six	Sex	*Sex*
Seven	Sju	*Syeu*
Eight	Åtta	*Ottah*
Nine	Nio	*Neo*
Ten	Tio	*Teo*
Twenty	Tjugo	*Tyeugoo*
Fifty	Femtio	*Fehmtee*
One hundred	Ett hundra	*Eht hundrah*
SIGNS & NOTICES		
Airport	Flygplats	*Flyhg-plahts*
Railway station	Tågstation	*Taeg-statioen*
Platform	Spår	*Spoer*
Smoking/No smoking	Rökning/Rökning Förbjudet	*Reuk-ning/Reuk-ning feurbjuhdet*
Toilets	Toaletten	*Toahlehtehn*
Ladies/Gentlemen	Damer/Herrar	*Dahmer/Hahrrahr*
Subway	Tunnelbana	*Tunael-baena*